D1445762

The Family in Post-Industrial America

AAAS Selected Symposia Series

Published by Westview Press
5500 Central Avenue, Boulder, Colorado

for the

American Association for the Advancement of Science
1776 Massachusetts Ave., N.W., Washington, D.C.

The Family in Post-Industrial America

Some Fundamental Perceptions for Public Policy Development

Edited by David Pearce Snyder

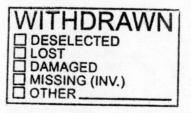
AAAS Selected Symposium **32**

AAAS Selected Symposia Series

Copyright © 1979 by the American Association for the Advancement of Science

Published in 1979 in the United States of America by
  Westview Press, Inc.
  5500 Central Avenue
  Boulder, Colorado 80301
  Frederick A. Praeger, Publisher

Library of Congress Cataloging in Publication Data
Main entry under title:
The Family in post-industrial America.
   (AAAS selected symposium; 32)
   Includes bibliographical references.
   1. Family--United States--Congresses.
2. Family policy--United States--Congresses.
I. Snyder, David Pearce. II. Series: American
Association for the Advancement of Science. AAAS
selected symposium; 32.
HQ535.F343   301.42'0973   79-5230
ISBN 0-89158-482-X

Printed and bound in the United States of America

About the Book

Traditional public policy toward the family, the authors
of this book argue, has produced an array of fragmented mechanical programs in response to specific, perceived "dys-
functions" in family performance. Policy has been biased by
a restrictive perception that families unlike the nuclear,
two-parent household are either ailing or aberrant.

In response to these observations, the authors portray
the family as a natural, ongoing, and dynamically adaptive
element of Western civilization. They suggest that legisla-
tors and policy analysts should view the household as a tangible social and economic asset and an appropriate technology
with which a number of tasks (such as child care, education,
health, disability and unemployment insurance, social security, and the welfare of the aged) now performed by more complex and costly formal institutions may be better accomplished.

About the Series

The *AAAS Selected Symposia Series* was begun in 1977 to
provide a means for more permanently recording and more
widely disseminating some of the valuable material which is
discussed at the AAAS Annual National Meetings. The volumes
in this *Series* are based on symposia held at the Meetings
which address topics of current and continuing significance,
both within and among the sciences, and in the areas in which
science and technology impact on public policy. The *Series*
format is designed to provide for rapid dissemination of
information, so the papers are not typeset but are reproduced
directly from the camera-copy submitted by the authors, without copy editing. The papers are organized and edited by
the symposium arrangers who then become the editors of the
various volumes. Most papers published in this *Series* are
original contributions which have not been previously published, although in some cases additional papers from other
sources have been added by an editor to provide a more comprehensive view of a particular topic. Symposia may be reports of new research or reviews of established work, particularly work of an interdisciplinary nature, since the AAAS
Annual Meetings typically embrace the full range of the
sciences and their societal implications.

WILLIAM D. CAREY
*Executive Officer
American Association for
the Advancement of Science*

Contents

About the Editor and Authors

David P. Snyder *is a senior planning officer with the U.S. Internal Revenue Service. His areas of specialization include personal, institutional, and community value systems and decision processes and information/communication technology. He is also associate director for sociopolitical forecasting programs, with the Industrial Management Center, Inc., and has served as an instructor in futures programs for the U. S. Civil Service Commission. He is also the editor of* Life-Styles Tomorrow, *president of the Washington, D.C. chapter of the World Future Society, and the author of numerous publications on the future, information systems, and social change.*

Catherine M. Allen, *an assistant professor of sociology and social work, Texas Tech University, specializes in the sociology of the family and social welfare policy. She has conducted family therapy in hospital and private agency settings, has presented papers on child abuse and wife abuse, and has served as a consultant on incest prevention. She was a consultant to the White House Conference on Families, evaluating the scope of federal research on the family, and she has also done research on a father's rights advocacy group.*

Kenneth E. Boulding *is a Distinguished Professor of Economics and director of the Program of Research on General Social and Economic Dynamics at the Institute of Behavioral Science, University of Colorado, Boulder. He has served as president of the American Economic Association and of the International Studies Association, is a member of the National Academy of Sciences, and is currently president of the American Association for the Advancement of Science. He has published widely in popular and scholarly journals and has written many books on economic policy and social dynamics, most recently* Stable Peace *(University of Texas, 1978). The recipient of many honors and awards, he is currently concerned with the area of general systems.*

Joseph F. Coates *is assistant to the director of the Office of Technology Assessment of the U. S. Congress and is a former program manager for technology assessment at the National Science Foundation. A chemist by training, his major current interest is planning for the future, with primary emphasis on the impact of technology on society. He has published numerous papers dealing with public affairs, technology assessment, military affairs, and criminal justice.*

Gregg Edwards, *presently manager of the National Science Foundation program New Knowledge for Productivity, was formerly assistant director for various science education programs at the Foundation. A physicist by training, he is active in numerous professional associations in physics, computer uses, and futures research.*

David A. Goslin *is the executive director of the Assembly of Behavioral and Social Sciences of the National Academy of Sciences. A sociologist by training, he has worked on many projects concerned with educational testing and technology and their social and ethical implications. He has been a special consultant to the College Board Commission on Testing, is a consultant to the* Encyclopedia Britannica *and to the Russell Sage Foundation, and is a member of many other advisory groups, including the Advisory Committee on Special Projects of the Center for Advanced Study in the Behavioral Sciences. He has published widely, particularly in the field of ethics, testing, and record-keeping in education, was the editor of* Handbook of Social-ization Theory *(Rand McNally, 1969), and prepared the film* A Place to Meet, A Way to Understand *(in collaboration with Urie Bronfenbrenner and Bert Pence) for the White House Conference on Children (1970).*

Carol B. Stack *is director of the Center for the Study of the Family and the State, Institute of Policy Sciences and Public Affairs, Duke University. An anthropologist by training, she is the author of several publications on family policy, including* All Our Kin: Strategies for Survival in a Black Community *(Harper & Row, 1974). She is a member of the National Academy of Sciences Task Force on Families and of the President's Mental Health Committee.*

Winifred I. Warnat *is a professor in the School of Education at American University and director of the Adult Learning Project, which focuses on the development of adult learning and training strategies.* She has been involved in many programs designed to meet the needs of the learning disabled and the handicapped, and has published articles dealing with these educational strategies. *Among her numerous publications are* LPS: A Life Process System for Stress Resolution *(in press) and* The Child Care Domain from an Educational Perspective *(Final Report, Teachers Corps Technical Assistance, U.S. Office of Education, 1978).*

Preface

This volume is based on a session presented at the 1978
AAAS Annual Meeting in Washington, D.C. As arranger of the
session, and as Editor of this volume, it has been my in-
tention to present a set of cogent observations and research
findings designed to inform the current public dialogue concerning the state of the family in our society, and in
particular, to broaden and integrate the context of that
dialogue.

In Chapter 1, Professor Kenneth Boulding describes three
fundamental types of human relationships and the modes of
resource allocation and economic transaction which characterize
each; within this context, Professor Boulding argues that all
three modes are essential to the functioning of society, and
that households possess characteristics which are uniquely
suited to the use of the most productive of these modes. In
Chapter 2, Dr. Catherine Allen examines the range of differing
definitions which various institutions and professions in our
society assign to the notion of "family," and posits the need
for a common definition which reflects the family's acknowledged social and economic functions.

Dr. Winifred Warnat (Chapter 3) presents a structured
model of the household as the ongoing center of affective
learning throughout the lives of each of its members. In
her paper, Dr. Warnat also proposes this process as the
logical basis for a "collaboration-of-equals" between families and formal education institutions in mounting an effective program of life-long cognitive learning.

Chapter 4, by Dr. Carol Stack, combines an assessment of
the historic variability of Western household forms and roles
with her own field work on the extended familial networks
of the urban poor, and finds these networks to be an effective evolutionary adaptation that is closer to the mainstream

of Western tradition than the diminishing nuclear family
form of the American middle class. And, in Chapter 5,
Dr. Gregg Edwards presents both a framework and a method-
ology, based upon a broad inter-disciplinary survey, by
which social policy may address families and familiar groups
as the continuously adapting source of social and economic
performance. Echoing and incorporating the perceptions of
the preceding authors, Dr. Edwards applies his hypotheses
to an analysis of the manners by which current social policy hampers that adaptivity at a time when fundamental
shifts in America's economic and technological environment
are encouraging such evolutionary change.

     In my own contribution to this volume (Chapter 6), I
offer an approach by which social policy might, in a practical and conservative manner, seek to encourage adaptive
initiatives by familiar groups to reassume some of the
responsibilities given over to public and private sector
institutions during the industrial revolution, thereby both
strengthening the family and reversing the long-term trend
toward institutional dependency in our society. Chapter 7
represents the summary comments made at the close of the
1978 AAAS session by Dr. David Goslin, who served as session
discussant. In his commentary, Dr. Goslin has framed a
clear statement of 5 critical issues or problems confronting
the contemporary family debate. For this reason, while
Dr. Goslin's remarks appear here in their proper chrono-
logical sequence, I would suggest that Chapter 7 be read
first, prior to the Introduction, as a most instructive
orientation to the body of thought contained in the volume.

     Chapter 8, by Joseph Coates, is based upon an address
delivered to the Maryland Chapter of the American Society
of Public Administration meeting at the headquarters of the
Social Security Administration in December, 1976. It is
included in this volume because, in his speculation on the
outlook for one of our more nearly universal institutional
social technologies, Mr. Coates suggests some fundamental
future realities confronting the Social Security system,
and how that system might, by way of forestalling some of
the problems implicit to those realities, become an effective force for revitalizing the family.

The Family in Post-Industrial America

Introduction

David P. Snyder

A fundamental aspect of modernization has been the growing specialization of individuals and institutions in our society. In the 1700's, one might receive a university degree in Medicine, Theology, Philosophy or Law; today, there are specific courses of learning for any one of several hundred specialized fields, from agronomy to zoology. Similarly, George Washington had only three cabinet-level offices to help with the management of the nation's domestic civilian affairs. Today, there are 11 such departments, each overseeing dozens of bureaus, with more on the way.

This increase in specialization is a natural phenomenon, reflecting both the growing size of our common national endeavor, and the complexification inherent to the evolution of human knowledge and enterprise. The mobilization of resources around specified tasks or purposes is a mode of operation that has stood Western civilization in good stead, and has permitted us to achieve unparalleled productivities and great goals. At the same time, the patent effectiveness of specialization--early postulated by theorists like Adam Smith and Charles Babbage and applied to institutions by Eli Whitney, Frank Gilbreth and others--has contributed substantially to the relatively narrow focus of commitment which characterizes our institutions.

In the private sector, the specialized commitment of institutions has led most organizations to ignore, or substantially discount, many of their obvious interactions with their social and ecological environment. In the public sector, specialization has led to the creation of multitudes of specialized programs, institutions, and policies, the simple existence of which further promotes more fragmented growth by increasingly pre-empting or confounding comprehensive approaches to public policy issues.

1

In assessing public policy on the family, we tend to be fragmented by just such institutional specializations. Congressional Committees on Aging, Human Development, Education, etc.--each holds hearings on the family as it relates to its particular concerns. Similarly, Executive Branch agencies and special commissions focus upon various aspects of family life, such as child health or single parent households; or upon various government programs affecting the family, like food stamps or welfare. State and local jurisdictions, their program structures extensively determined by Federal standards, generally follow suit in their efforts at policy analysis, legislative review or program evaluation.

Such narrowly focused assessments are essential for evaluating specific programs or problems, but they provide neither sufficient insight nor appropriate orientation for examining overall public policy toward the family as an institution. This is because such efforts fail to address the family's basic social and economic functions. The family is the fundamental productive unit of our society; it produces labor for the market place, and citizens for the community and the polity.

In 1976, for example, America's families paid over $115 billion in income tax, while by comparison, corporations paid approximately $47 billion in taxes, and single taxpayers only accounted for $25 billion in Federal revenues. Moreover, while roughly one-half of the nation's 11 million individually-owned businesses had adjusted gross incomes of less than $10,000 per annum in 1975, almost 30 million families had annual adjusted gross incomes in excess of that amount. In that same year, more than one-half of all American corporations--approximately 1.2 million firms--reported assets of less than $100,000, while an estimated 3 million U.S. households have assets in excess of that amount. Thus, in terms of their operating expenditures and their capital investments, families collectively represent our single most important economic institution, but are not recognized as such by our public policy.

Similarly, research by the social sciences has made abundantly clear the dominant role of the family in determining the educational achievement of the young, and in teaching the behavioral skills and social values which are critical to the functioning and maturation of our society. Yet no significant public policies support the family in these functions. Rather, public policy tends to promote the performance of these functions by larger, formal institutions, such as schools or public television.

The current reexamination of our public policy toward the family must take these realities into account, or we may fail to serve <u>either</u> our families or our nation. Unfortunately, a review of current policy analysis activities, particularly at the Federal level, does not reflect such a comprehensive orientation. In 1977, for example, family sociologist Catherine Allen of American University conducted a survey of the definitions of family employed by various Federal programs, in an attempt to develop a common, multi-dimensional definition for use throughout government. Upon completing her research, she circulated her initial proposal to a number of Federal organizations for comment. In responding to the proposed new definition, which is discussed in the second chapter of this book, one HEW agency replied that it reflected inappropriate economic criteria, and that it "had probably been developed by the Department of Labor."

This volume is a challenge to such pernicious policy fragmentation. In the papers that follow, my associates discuss some fundamental realities which relate to the functions of families and familiar groups in our society, in an attempt to suggest an appropriate context within which to conduct a meaningful family policy debate.

The Market and the Budget in Perspective

1

The Economics of Human Relationships in the Household and in the Society

Kenneth E. Boulding

Human beings cannot get along without perspective, that property both of the senses and of our images of fact and of value which makes the near look larger, demand our attention more insistently and be more highly valued than the far. The near seems big and imminent, and impresses itself on our attention; it is therefore not surprising that the near is dear and is more highly valued than the far. As we expand our intellectual capacity to develop realistic images of the universe--that is, the totality of reality--we come to recognize that perspective is in some sense an illusion of perception. We understand that the person right next to us whose image covers a large part of our retina, is in fact no larger than the person a mile away whom we can barely see.

Perspective in values is a much trickier problem. Indeed, it underlies many of the dilemmas and unresolved anxieties of social life. We can postulate an objective system of evaluation which denies value perspective, in which the distant is seen to be just as important and as valuable as the close. It is this perception which has led prophets and religious leaders to advocate universal love, and even like Noyes and the Oneida Community, to deprecate "particular love." There is reason in this, for if perspective is an illusion in the world of fact, why is it not an illusion in the world of values?

Perspective, Perception and Social Evolution

There are, infact, profound evolutionary reasons, both for the existence of perspective and also, oddly enough, for the larger perception that it is an illusion. It is our immediate environment in which we have to survive, so survival involves getting messages from what is close to us. Furthermore, there is a physical principle that the intensity of a message, like a light wave which emanates uniformly in all

directions from a single source, must be proportional to the
reciprocal of the square of the distance from that source.
At one foot from the source, the message is distributed over
a sphere one foot in diameter. At ten feet, it is distributed over a sphere ten feet in diameter, which is one hundred
times the area of the one-foot sphere, and the intensity
therefore is only one hundredth at ten feet what it is at one
foot. This principle applies to the three senses that enable
us to perceive at a distance--sight, hearing and smell. Perspective applies even more dramatically to touch and taste,
where actual contact is necessary for perception, and the
most minute distance between the source and the perceptor
destroys the perception altogether.

Attention involves the evaluation of perceptions. Some
perceptions are interpreted as more important than others and
we "attend" to these. When we are driving a car we perceive
our environment almost subconsciously until we see a flashing
red light. There are good evolutionary reasons for this
property also. Some things in the environment are inimical
to survival, like predators, and it clearly helps not only to
perceive them but to perceive them attentively. Other elements in our environment assist survival, like food, and
these we also perceive attentively, and value, in the sense
that we accept rather than avoid them.

The evolution of love and altruism is something which
has puzzled the sociobiologists, but it is clearly in the
record. The development of sexual reproduction clearly would
have been impossible unless there had not also developed in
the genetic structures potential for the attractiveness of
sexual union. The biological advantages of the greater
variability, and wide gene pool which sexual reproduction
affords, must have been very large indeed to compensate for
the extraordinary inconvenience of having to get two members
of opposite sexes together in an act of copulation. Sexual
attraction need not be mutual and certainly does not require
affection, as in the case of the female spider that eats the
male who has just fertilized her. Similarly, there is the
puzzle as to why the male is more commonly attracted to the
female than the female to the male. Certainly one sex must
put a high value on copulating with the other if sexual reproduction is not to collapse.

Parental care perhaps represents the evolutionary begin-
nings of love as reflected in altruism; that is, behavior
that benefits another at the cost of injury to the self.
Sociobiologists have argued that altruism will not have survival value genetically unless the beneficiary carries at
least some of the genes of the benefactor. There are possi-

ble exceptions to this in terms of the survival of group cultures. In any case, there are good evolutionary reasons why
the near should be dear, not only in spacial propinquity, but
also in kinship.

The situation is enormously complicated as we move into
human history. With the development of the human race, what
I have called "noogenetic" evolution assumes overwhelming importance. There are really two genetic structures which develop in the course of evolution: one is the biogenetic
structure coded and transmitted in DNA and the genes; the
other is the noogenetic, which consists of learned structures
in nervous systems or other biogenetically-produced appara-
tuses which are capable of receiving structure from inputs of
information. These learned structures, like the genes, are
transmitted from one generation to the next, but by a learning process, not by bio-chemical replication. We see this
certainly in the birds who have to learn part of their bird
song; it may even exist in lower forms of life, though we are
not sure of that.

Noogenetics is of overwhelming importance in the human
race. The human baby comes into the world biogenetically
provided with a brain which is capable of receiving enormous
complexity of structure in the course of the individual's
life. The biogenetic difference between the humans that
lived fifty thousand years ago and those alive now is very
small indeed. But the noogenetic difference is enormous. It
took fifty thousand years of learning and transmissions of
knowledge, including values, to produce the complexity of the
world as we know it today.

As we move through noogenetic evolution, the survival
value of perspective diminishes, and of the perception that
perspective is an illusion increases. This is because as
knowledge grows, the behavior of human beings affects larger
and larger areas both in space and in time. Consequently,
those cultures in which the sense of perspective has been
very strong--which have neither known nor cared about what
lay over the hill and in which the near has been all that has
been perceived and all that has been valued--have declined,
often to extinction. Those cultures have prospered which
have expanded their noogenetic structures--that is, their
images of the world and the values placed on it--so that they
have fewer illusions of perspective, and therefore see the
world more realistically in terms of space and time; perhaps
even in terms of values. It was those cultures in which perspective was seen as illusion that became conquerors. The
Romans, for instance, thought not merely of Rome but of the
whole of the Mediterranean as their home. They made Roman

citizens out of people who were not related to them by blood, or as we should say today, by genes. The Romans were neither lovable nor very loving, but they had in some degree, relative to the people around them, especially the Greeks, a less illusionary social perspective.

Perceiving Our Fellows, Near and Far

At this point the reader may well ask, what has all this got to do with the family or the household in relation to the larger society? The answer is, of course, that it all depends on the reader's sense of perspective! In the light of the larger, social perspective, the relation between the sense of perspective itself and the character, role, and function of the household is very close. In terms of perspective, every individual is the center of a perceptual universe. There is an image in each individual's mind as to where he or she is in relation to the whole surrounding world. We are each surrounded by a set of spheres of which we are the centermost, and this is as true of social space as it is of physical space. Certain things are very near--our own bodies, the clothes we are wearing, the chair we are sitting in; some things a little further--the building we are in, the landscape that surrounds it; some things are still further-- the nearest city, our country, the earth; until we get to the solar system and the universe.

In social space too, if any individual is given a list of names of people who are familiar or about whom something is known, almost everyone could arrange these names in a rough order of closeness. There may be more than one dimension of closeness. We could range people on a scale of caring, specified perhaps in regard to malevolence or benevolence. This is the question as to how far our perception of the welfare of another affects our perception of our own welfare. There is benevolence if our perception of an increase in the welfare of another increases our own welfare. There is malevolence if our perception of an increase in the welfare of another diminishes our own welfare. There is indifference if we perceive that a variation in another's welfare does not affect our own welfare at all. Both those toward whom we feel benevolent and malevolent may be seen as close; those to which we are indifferent are distant.

Similarly, we may have a dimension of power. We could arrange people in our environment roughly by the amount of power we have over them or the amount of power they have over us. The two orders are likely to be different. We may feel that we have very little power over the President of the United States, but that he has a good deal of power over us.

The point is that our perceptions group themselves in a very
complex way into overlapping sets, some of which have fairly
clear boundaries and others do not. We are, for instance,
likely to have a fairly clear set of perceptions concerning
those who are related to us by kinship, even out to fourth
cousins.

Of course, the kinship set is not wholly uniform or precise, because some cultures define kinship differently from
others. But in most cultures two people will not identify
themselves as kin unless they have a common ancestor or a
common descendant. In some cultures, the kin also include
those who are regarded as kin in a genetic sense. These
might be called "collateral kin," of which the spouse is the
closest, but which may also include spouses and kin of
spouses of genetically related kin. In some cultures, there
may be adopted or conventional kin who are not genetically
related in any way. These relationship patterns have been
the delight of anthropologists; they constitute a remarkable
universal human perception which is, as far as we know, virtually unique to the human race and which reflects again the
remarkable extension of perspective of which the human race
is capable. I doubt if any non-human animal possesses even
the concept of a grandparent.

The concept of a household is fuzzier than that of kin.
It could be defined, of course, as all those who live in the
same house or dwelling, which again could almost be defined
as any set of spaces which has a front door which can be
shut. A household, of course, often contains people who are
not kin and are not even regarded as part of the family, such
as servants who live in. The family, furthermore, can contain members who are not biological kin, such as adopted
children, There are, of course, legal and administrative
definitions, which Dr. Allen discusses, but these merely
help to define the family and household legally and adminis-
tratively; they do not purport to define it sociologically,
conceptually or functionally.

There is a vague boundary between the household and the
extended household, just as there is between the family and
the extended family. The extended household may include a
rather close penumbra of the household--people who are always
welcome, who drop in and out, for whom a room is kept, and so
on. Beyond this we get a circle of friends and acquaint-
ances; the outermost limit is perhaps represented by the list
of people to whom we send Christmas or holiday greetings,
which may be as many as three or four hundred. Intersecting
this set is another set of work mates, the people with whom
we are close when we are out of the house, and who may or may

not belong to the extended household, but who mostly, one
suspects, do not. Similar intersecting sets may be found in
the church, in clubs, in sports, in schools, colleges, alumni
associations, political associations, and so on. Every organization that we belong to at least abuts onto the extended
household.

All this is important for the general organization of
society because the type of relationship that we find among
the near is different from what we find among the far. If we
try to look at society--that is, human history as it spreads
out through time and space (free from the illusions of perspective)--we can see it first as a vast, ongoing, evolutionary process which involves constant change in the total noogenetic structure, or "noosphere," as de Chardin called it;
that is, the total body of structured knowledge, know-how and
values in the minds of all persons on the earth. This process takes place through a constant process of mutation; that
is, the generation of new ideas, new values, which may or may
not spread by a learning process. We see also a forgetting
process through aging or the extinction of cultures and concepts, and so on.

The noosphere may reasonably be seen as the origin of a
continual process of production, which produces first of all
material artifacts--houses, clothing, furniture, food, and so
on--most of which are commodities that enter into exchange.
We see also the production of organizations; for instance, a
new family by marriage, or a new corporation by incorporation,
a new religion by a prophet, a new state by independence, and
so on. Then we also have the production of persons themselves, which are produced partly by the inputs which they
receive from others, partly of course from their biogenetic
information structure, and partly from the self-generated
information of the human brain.

Allocating Artifacts and Transacting Society's Business

Within this ongoing evolutionary process there are a
number of sub-systems by which resources are allocated, or
roles and tasks are assigned, and products are made. I have
elsewhere distinguished three basic types of relationships by
which roles and organizational structures are created. One
is the threat, in which A says to B, "You do something that
I want or I will do something that you do not want." Another
is exchange, in which A says to B, "You do something that I
want and I will do something that you want." The third is
the integrative relationship, in which A says to B, "You do
something because of what you are and what I am, and because
of the system which comprises both of us."

Upon these three fundamental types of human relationships, society has based three organized relationships, patterns or systems. The first is the <u>market</u>, which is the complex network of exchange, and which fits within a framework
of organizations--laws, customs, and so on--which also require elements of both threat and integrative relationships.
(The perfect market beloved of economists is, of course, a
fiction, although a very useful fiction, as it is often useful to have an abstract model from which the real world is
perceived as a deviation.) Within the imperfect markets of
the real world, transactions are continually going on at
prices (exchange ratios) which vary all the time but which do
have a certain central tendency towards a range of equilib-
rium values. With given techniques, there is some set of
relative prices at which perceived distributions of welfare
are such that there is no net tendency for persons or organizations to move away from one occupation into another. This
is the "natural price" system of Adam Smith, which has quite
legitimately dominated economic thought ever since its enun-
ciation.

Now, I believe it would be useful, at this juncture, to
discuss a simple example of the market system in operation,
by supposing that there were a sudden, massive change in
public consumption patterns. Let us suppose, for instance,
that half the population converted to Mormonism and refused
to consume alcohol, tea or coffee. The prices of liquor, tea
and coffee would decline very sharply. This would make their
production unprofitable. People and organizations would
leave the production of these things and move into other occupations, the demand for the products of which would have
expanded as a result of people increasing their purchases of
other things besides alcohol, tea and coffee. The industries
which produce alcoholic beverages, tea and coffee would decline and others would correspondingly grow, until the relative prices of alcoholic beverages, tea and coffee were sufficient to afford a return to the occupations which produced
them, which would not induce any further net movement out of
them. The relative prices of alcoholic beverages, tea and
coffee might actually be lower than before if the now smaller
industry were concentrated on lower cost producers, as it
would likely be. The great virtue of the market system is
that it minimizes the necessity for specific agreements. It
operates simply by each individual or organization changing
its activities in directions which promise better overall
returns.

Now, however, when we look at organizations and the organization members which make the exchanges and which constitute the intra-organizational marketplace, we find a different

principle at work, particularly where there are more than two
people involved in an organization. An organization consists
of a structured set of roles arranged very largely through a
central budget. Money, let us say, is received through
various members of the organization, either in exchange for
products, goods or services, or as one-way transfers, such as
taxes or gifts, but it is at the disposal of the central
decision-making authority of the organization—e.g., dic-
tator, legislature, board of directors or trustees, etc.
This authority is often delegated to one or more executives
or managers, subject to recall if performance is found to be
unsatisfactory. The basic organizing principle in an organization is the budget approved by the central authority, by
which the available resources are transferred, first perhaps
to subordinate managers in departments, and ultimately to
those who purchase the goods or the labor services which
are required to make the organization function.

The budget represents an allocation of power throughout
the organization, and to a large extent, an allocation of
effective decision-making authority. These are not quite the
same thing. Some organizations have very "tight" budgets, in
which the purpose for which each item is to be used is clearly specified and there is very little distribution of decision-making authority. Other organizations have "loose"
budgets, in which people to whom the budgets allocate funds
have a certain latitude in how to spend them.

The third pattern by which society is structured, in
addition to the market and the budget, is the grant or one-
way transfer from one person or organization to another.
This differs from the budget, in that it takes place between
organizations rather than within them. It differs from
exchange in that it is a one-way transfer, whereas exchange
is a two-way transfer. A grant involves a real redistribu-
tion of net worth of some sort, whereas exchange involves
redistributions of assets, but not of net worth, if the
assets are assumed to be of equal value. If I give you $100
and you give me $100 worth of potatoes, our assets are redis-
tributed but our net worths are unchanged. If you give me
$100 and I give you nothing but a smile and a handshake, my
accountant would reckon that your net worth is $100 less and
mine is $100 more.

The grant is a particularly important form of transaction within households and families. On the whole, we give
grants to those who are in some sense "near." This may mean
near in terms of kinship, as in the grants given by parents
to children, and in later life often by children to parents
and grandparents. It may mean near in sheer physical propin-

quity within the household, where we get grants to and from
people living in the same household even when they are not
kin. It may also mean near in terms of nearness of interest
or concern. Grants are given by individuals to charities, to
churches, to political organizations, with which the individual identifies; to things that are close to the individual
in terms of concerns and interests about the world. Unco-
erced grants emerge out of benevolence. A is more likely to
give a grant to B if he perceives an increase in B's welfare
also increases A's welfare. We may also get negative grants
arising out of malevolence; injuries done by A to individual
or organization B, where a decline in the welfare of B is
perceived by A to increase A's welfare.

Now, somewhere between grants and exchange there is
another phenomenon of particular importance in the household,
and this is reciprocity. Reciprocity is a mutual exchange of
grants. A gives something to B out of the goodness of A's
heart; B gives something to A out of the goodness of B's
heart. Reciprocity differs from exchange in that it is non-
contractual, and whatever accounting may be involved is informal, even subconscious. Such exchanges do not originate
by A saying to B, "You give me something and I will give you
something." On the other hand, mutual grants are similar to
exchanges in that they have "terms," which are each party's
expectations or perceptions of how much they get per unit of
what they give. In exchange, these terms are fairly visible
and objective. When I buy a shirt, the money which I give up
is very much the same money as what the storekeeper receives.
The shirt which he gives up is the same shirt that I receive (1).

In a reciprocal relationship, on the other hand, the
terms may be perceived very differently by the two parties.
In a marriage, for instance, each spouse may think that they
are giving a great deal and not getting very much, or that
they are not giving very much and getting a great deal, depending on the nature of what might be called the "reciprocal
product," which can be either a net benefit or a net loss to
both parties depending on the nature of their relationship
and their perceptions of it.

Within any household, reciprocity is a key relationship.
The allocation of an enormous amount of family activity is
simply "understood" by the various parties; that A will do
one thing and that B will do another. If one of the parties
in a household should come to feel that the overall terms of
reciprocity are inadequate or unfair, this introduces a
strain in the relationship. It may eventually lead to a
breakup, a divorce, a child running away from home, even, in

extreme cases, murder. One of the great problems of reciprocity is that it is largely tacit and understood. Thus, it is hard to communicate about it, and it is particularly hard to renegotiate the terms of reciprocity.

This, of course, is largely what marriage counselors are all about. Industrial conciliators and negotiators are also extensively concerned with this problem, since the labor relationship involves a great deal of reciprocity as well as exchange. The work the employee gives up is a sacrifice of the alternative uses of time, plus perhaps certain disutilities associated with the work itself. What the employer receives is the product of the work. What the employer gives up is the alternative uses of the money paid. What the worker receives is the purchasing power of that money. It is not surprising that this is a relationship which is hard to negotiate. Similarly,what the husband may give up in a nuclear family household is certain alternative uses of his time, money and emotional resources. What the wife receives is certain security, perhaps a certain leisure, a certain amount of money, certain satisfactions of sex, status, and so on. Similarly, what the wife gives up is a certain independence, certain uses of time, certain relationships with other people. What the husband receives is a "home," a shelter from the world, meals, affection, certain sexual enjoyments, and so on. Whether the terms of reciprocity for both parties are positive depends on the joint reciprocity product--that which is created because of a relationship which neither would have had otherwise. This is often neglected in discussions of the household. It is all too often assumed that reciprocity must be a zero-sum game; that what one gains, the other loses. In reality, quite to the contrary, we have ample evidence to suggest that, unless a household functions as a positive-sum game, it is highly likely not to work at all.

We have to worry if the joint reciprocity product of the household becomes less than what might be called its "social product." This is something very hard to estimate but also something very real. The social product of the household includes, for instance, children, their rearing, and a fair amount of their education, the learning of language, socialization into the ethos of the larger community, and so on. Often it involves caring for the aged or the sick, for those afflicted with other misfortunes--accidents, disabilities, unemployment, bad harvests, and so on. It sometimes involves taking care of the mentally ill, even of criminals. In sum, the household performs something of the functions of the school, the church, the hospital, the mental institution, the prison, and is surely the primary organization responsible for sustaining the existing human population, and replacing it as it ages and dies. This social product--on which the very continued existence of society depends--is only produced because there is a joint reciprocity product of the household sufficient to insure its continuance. If this declines beyond a certain point households will break up, refuse to have or to care for children and will raise a defective or insufficient next generation, will not provide nurturance and support for the handicapped and the other institutions of society, then government, private charity, and so on, may not be able to take up the slack.

The Social Product of the Household

The social product of the household can perhaps be visualized most clearly if we imagine a society without this institution. We can imagine a society in which everybody lives in a hotel or dormitory, in which marriage is prohibited, in which sex is taken care of by masturbation or prostitution, in which children are conceived and born in special institutions designed for the purpose, and raised and educated in other institutions outside the family; a society in which the care of the sick is all done in hospitals or by visiting nurses, in which the aged are all taken care of in public or commercial institutions, in which all children are placed in boarding schools, in which nobody knows or wants to know who his genetic mother and father were, or his kin, and so on. In short, a society in which each individual is dependent upon, and responsible to, only him- or herself, or some formal, structured institution.

Such a society is certainly conceivable. It has never been realized and seems unlikely to be realized, at least in the near future, simply because the household has--and always has had--such a large role, both for the individuals within it and for the society, that the total substitution of its role seems to be merely absurd. The reason for the historical success and persistence of the household, however, has been the existence of perspective. It is the near who have been dear. It is almost exclusively within the household that love and benevolence have been generated in any quantity; and it is only within the household that the grants economy and the mutual reciprocity which has been necessary for human survival and the survival of any society, particularly as applied to children, has been able to develop.

There is little doubt that, in the last 100 years or so, there has been an important movement to reassign at least some of the functions of the traditional household to larger-scale institutions, particularly centering around the national state. We see this perhaps in its extreme form in communism, which in a certain sense represents a movement on the part of the national state to take over most of the "social production" functions of the household. Of course, it never really goes this far, for even in the communist countries the household is still of great importance. After its initial period, for instance, Russian communism reemphasized the importance of the household, the strength of the marriage tie, and discouraged casual and Bohemian ways of life. It became, indeed, almost as Victorian as Marx himself.

In the capitalist countries, there has been a great rise in the functions and powers of the state with the development of social democracy, and many functions which were previously regarded as essentially the province of the family or the household have been assumed, at least in part, by the state. These include social insurance, caring of the aged, medical care, education of the child, income maintenance, and so on. Indeed, it could be argued that the family or the household is under greater active attack from the state in the capitalist countries than it is in the communist countries, since the erosion is more subtle and less conscious. On the other hand, there has also been in these societies an increase in the variety of households. And, although we probably have still not attained the extraordinary variety of households which characterized Europe in the Middle Ages, we do have increasing numbers of communes of various kinds, producer cooperatives, homosexual households, religious communities like the Society of Brothers and monasteries, and so on.

Coordinating Collective Enterprise--
Households vs. Hierarchies

A critical question today, both with regard to family policy and to many other social and economic issues, is that of the optimum scale of organizations of various types. The household, and still more the family, is an organization within which there has to be a great deal of interaction among the parties, and where, as we have seen, reciprocity is the rule, as opposed to the contract. Beyond a fairly small scale--say, of 5 to 10 people--the efficiency of this type of organization declines very sharply, simply because the larger the number of people who are in these informal relationships, the more time has to be spent in the interaction among different pairs and subsets of the group, and even among the whole group. The number of possible pairs, for instance, rises very rapidly as the number of individuals in this kind of relationship increases. Two people, of course, are only one pair; 10 people can have 45 possible pairs, 120 possible trios; with 100 people, we get 4,950 possible pairs, and so on. The price of community is palaver--meetings, discussions, interactions--which increases very rapidly as the size of the community grows. The family, I have sometimes said, is as much community as I can take, at least at this intense level.

Once we go beyond the immediate household to the extended family, and to the "non-kin" extended family which we find in church groups, clubs, work places, and so on, the relationships become less intimate and more generalized as the number of people in the group increases. The experience, even of the most idealistic and religiously motivated communities, like the Society of Brothers, suggests that a community of 200 people which organizes itself mainly through complex and loving relationships, has very little time to do anything else. Ultimately, the community becomes almost completely self-absorbed in running its own affairs, and is generally forced to adopt a great deal of informal hierarchy in order to survive.

Hierarchy has traditionally been the most accepted solution to the problem of the multiplication of communications as the size of the group grows. Hierarchy channels communications into patterns that resemble something like an organization chart, although even in hierarchical organizations, informal communications outside the chart still play a very important role. Hierarchy itself is subject to certain corruptions. Information is distorted as it goes from the bottom of the hierarchy, where it is usually collected, up to the top, where it is acted upon. I have elsewhere defined an organization as a hierarchy of wastebaskets--information is filtered out as it goes up the hierarchy, and very often what is really needed at the top has been filtered out somewhere along the way. Where the hierarchy is marked by dominance and by the threat power of the upper members over the lower members, information is even more distorted than normal, for it is often in the immediate or short-term interests of the lower-echelon members to distort it (a pathological disfunction brought on by the artificially enforced perspective inherent to threat-driven environments).

There are also disfunctions involved in the role-filling process of most hierarchies. This is the famous Peter principle--that people get promoted up to the point where they are incompetent (2). It is the principle also that people get promoted by pleasing their superiors, which is by no means a good preparation for occupying those superiors' roles. With all the disadvantages of hierarchy, however, it seems to work at least middling well, for its capacity to economize on communication permits much larger human organization than would otherwise be possible; note for instance

the size of the Soviet Union, which is the world's largest
brontosaurus.

It is the great virtue of the market that it permits the
coordination of very large numbers of people through specialization and exchange, without having to set up an organizational hierarchy which comprises all of them. However, there
is a tendency to develop organizations, even large-scale
organizations like General Motors, within the framework of
the market system. Market coordination may, of course,
break down, as it did in the Great Depression, through defla-
tion; or it can become somewhat pathological, as it does in
inflation. But when it works, it works pretty well over the
range of private goods, appropriable resources, and things
that are not easily monopolized. The market, of course, has
its own pathologies as everything does. It can be distorted
by monopoly, though the actual amount of such distortion is
not really very great. It produces a distribution of welfare
which may be regarded as unacceptable, and it therefore needs
offsets in the shape of a grants economy of one-way transfers, which on the whole is very inefficiently done in most
societies, but which may have considerable potential for
improvement.

Another great advantage of the market, as we have noted,
is that it economizes agreement. Informal communities have
to expend a great deal of time in getting agreement, while in
large organizations, agreement is often imposed from the top.
This imposition may be perceived as legitimate if other
things are perceived as worse, or it may be perceived as tyrannical. Where competition is imperfect--where there is
public or private monopoly--individuals' wants may, of
course, not be adequately supplied if the market edges over
into a system of dominance and imposition of agreement (for
instance, through persuasive advertising). Monopolies of
coercion and of persuasion are, however, much more likely to
arise in a centrally-planned economy, which is almost bound
to be tyrannical, simply because it really requires agreement
which cannot be freely reached in regard to the plan--the
budget--of the society, so the plan has to be largely imposed
by the authorities.

Back to Perspective

Many of the great debates which are shaking the human
race in the twentieth century can be interpreted as debates
about how to handle social and moral perspective. In particular, how to recognize and reconcile the perspective view of
life--that the near are dear--with the anti-perspective
view--that the earth is a spaceship with a crew of over four

billion, each of which ideally should be regarded as equally
significant and in which none can be excluded from the circle
of concern. One can interpret the great rise in the functions of the state and the increased proportion of the econ-
omy--and especially of the grants economy--which they absorb,
as in part a result of the development of an anti-perspective
point of view, which says that everybody should be dear,
whether genetically or physically near or not. Up to now,
"everybody" has generally included only people within national states, which seem to have inherited the functions of the
family as an exclusive field of concern, in the bounty of
which non-citizens should not share. On the other hand, the
development of things like the missionary movement, foreign
aid, and military intervention suggest a tendency toward the
expansion of the field of concern beyond the national state,
eventually to a world community. But the diseases of the
national state itself, particularly its tendency to break
down into war, are undermining its legitimacy at the same
time that it benefits from the declining legitimacy of the
household and the inability of small, informal, private
groups to solve the problems of a society of larger interaction.

    As we move towards one world, the need to think about
the total system with a minimum amount of perspective becomes
ever more pressing. In 900 A.D. the Mayan Empire could collapse without the emperor of China or Charlemagne ever hearing about it, much less having to be concerned about it. Now
a decision in Peking, Moscow or Washington, or even in Jeru-
salem or Pretoria, may shake the whole world to its founda-
tions. One world is terribly more dangerous than many
worlds, because if anything goes wrong, everything goes
wrong. Clearly, our current circumstances necessitate a
diminution of the illusions of perspective. This can only be
accomplished if the levels and types of organizations for
different sizes and numbers of people in interaction are
appropriate. If a one-world system is not to end in catas-
trophe, everybody in it must love everybody a little. It
need only be very little, but there must be a little more
than indifference and a lot more than malevolence would
imply. But we probably cannot love everybody a little
unless we love somebody a lot. Love and community are
learned mainly in the family and in the household, with a
little perhaps in the schools and in the church, but practically none at all in the marketplace or in the hierarchy.

    Even in the one-world system, therefore, there must be
some place for the household and the small community, where
we can know people personally and establish complex relationships and integrative structures, for what is learned in the

household is of overwhelming importance in determining the
general ethos and spirit of a society. Authoritarian households, it has often been pointed out, tend to produce authoritarian societies, and disorganized households may produce
disorganized societies. What people learn in school and in
church and through the media will, of course, reflect how
they both teach and learn in the household.   There is an
immensely complex process of interaction here which we understand very imperfectly. What we do know, however, is that
the larger society cannot be "like" a household any more
than a household can be like the larger society. If we try
to run a large society by love and preaching, we will end up
in tyranny; if we try to run a household by contract, it will
end up as a house of ill fame.

The future of the human race, then, may well rest on our
ability to perceive, to reconcile, and to integrate the
unique capabilities of the different levels of organization
at which we must operate. Without lively and creative households and families, society becomes a mechanical desert,
dependent entirely upon rules and hierarchies. Without the
larger perspective which only a commitment to the total
world order can satisfy (both as a fundamental assumption
and an overarching objective), the family and the household
can become pathological, producing individuals whose failure
of commitment to the larger world will lead to acts that
destroy it, and destroy the families and the households
along with it.

References and Notes

1. Even in this case the significance to the two parties of
    the objects exchanged may be different; indeed, must be
    different or there would have been no exchange at all.
    Exchange which is uncoerced can only take place if each
    party perceives that what is taken in is of greater
    value than what is given out, at least at the moment
    that the transaction occurs.
2. Laurence Peter and Raymond Hull, The Peter Principle
    (Bantam, New York, 1970).

Defining the Family for Post-Industrial Public Policy

Catherine M. Allen

Family life provides a binding force for our social system by training -- and moderating -- the individual. With such obvious political overtones, "family" finds itself with a wide range of definitions, each of which suits the needs and ends of those who command the definitions. Today, the most widely recognized American family model is the "nuclear family." But on close examination, we find that this view of the family encompasses several arbitrary -- and possibly obsolete -- assumptions.

The assumptions giving rise to the nuclear family concept include: a heterosexual, legally binding relationship between two adults; the adults' legal offspring; a common and private residential arrangement; and a distribution of authority which, while sometimes espousing democracy, is by and large patriarchal. There are serious questions as to whether these assumptions provide an accurate representation of how most people today live, or whether they are used merely to preserve traditional values.

It is the task of social scientists to evaluate demographic data on families and to test the nuclear model and its assumptions against empirical data. However, the primary sources of family data are constrained by the very conceptual dilemmas currently in question; the U.S. Census Bureau collects massive amounts of data by means of research questions and analyses that reflect both an absence of crucial indices, and a reliance on obsolete or biased concepts, producing a limited description at best. Moreover, observers with different and opposite ideologies agree that the nuclear family model, even if it provided an accurate description, fails to explain perceived changes in modern family life and in our society as a whole.

How is the Family Political?

In exploring the political implications of accepting
as valid the modern definition of nuclear family and of
viewing it as average and mainstream, we can see this clearly
born out by the following excerpt from a March 15, 1977,
Labor Department inter-office memo:

> The major thrust of any program ought to be to
> support this (nuclear family) as the predominant
> institution. The incentives should be arranged
> so that individuals prefer the two-parent arrange-
> ment. The earnings at work should be sufficiently
> greater than the dole or welfare to encourage
> women who are single parents to remarry. (1)

The Federal government's endorsement of the nuclear-
family-as-norm is not limited to the confines of private
intradepartmental memos. The Bureau of Labor Statistics
(BLS), in a recent Washington Post article, publicly lamented
its difficulties in making Americans' lifestyles fit into
established BLS models. James Rowe wrote on July 6, 1977:

OTHER PAY FOR HALF OF JOBLESS

> Fewer than half of the 7.3 million persons
> unemployed in the first three months of 1977
> lived in households in which no one else -- such
> as a spouse or child -- has a job, according to new
> data developed by the Bureau of Labor Statistics.
>
> Of the 7.8 million who were unemployed,
> 6.7 million lived in families and 1.1 million
> did not, although even all these persons did not
> live alone since unrelated individuals living
> together are not counted as a family for statis-
> tical purposes.
>
> The new data, presented in an article in
> the July Monthly Labor Review by deputy BLS com-
> missioner Janet L. Norwood, indicate that 41.8
> per cent of all unemployed individuals were in
> households in which they were the only wage
> earner.
>
> In families, only 32.2 per cent of the
> unemployed were the sole sources of income.

Norwood said that the new BLS data focus more on the relationship of the individual "to the people with whom they live" than did the old approach. Most BLS data gathering has been concerned with an average family, usually headed by a male who has a wife and two children.

The "average" family is a limited concept today because of the increased numbers of single-parent families and families with more than one wage earner.

Norwood cautions that the average family is more important "than statistics suggest, because many American families do pass through this stage. Nevertheless, policies dealing with the family must take account of the increasing variety of family types."

She noted that the "number of families with more than one earner is now larger than the number of single-earner families."

Last year there were 15.6 million single-earner families -- most of them with the husband the sole wage earner -- while there were 19.7 million with two earners and 7.2 million with three or more earners.

The data on the number of unemployed persons in families in which they are not the sole source of income seem to bear out what many economists have argued for a while: that the overall unemployment numbers reported each month may overstate economic hardship.

According to the BLS, the unemployment rate for women whose husbands have jobs was 6.4 per cent, while the unemployment rate for women with unemployed husbands was 18.8 per cent.

Of the 418,000 unemployed women who headed families with no husband present, however, almost 82 per cent were the sole wage earner. There were nearly 2 million unemployed husbands during the first quarter, 51.6 per cent of whom were the only wage earner.

Notice that, even though Norwood admits that the "average family," as defined by the nuclear model, today represents

a "limited concept," it can be justified to the extent that
"many American families do pass through this stage." Can
we not expect to have government policy address more than
a "stage" through which "many American families" pass? Although it is widely recognized that there is an "increasing
variety of family types," no adequate alternative model is
being acknowledged, or even seriously assessed, in the main.
Yet Norwood recognizes that "policies dealing with the
family must take account of" this increasing variety.

Turning Theory into Public Policy

Public policy -- to justify itself -- must use concepts which:
a) appear to represent established or traditional
perceptions of reality;
b) are pliable within statistical realms;
c) meet with some acceptable level of executive,
legislative, and public approval.
Academicians, on the other hand, can use more theoretical
freedom, and are therefore able to transcend some of the
limitations placed on policy makers. Of course, the true
task is to achieve the most productive blending of theory
in action.

Most academic thinking has coalesced along the lines
of 1) describing the organizational "structure" of the
family group and/or 2) analyzing the services or "functions"
the family performs for the larger society. It should be
pointed out that within "functions" of the family there is
a wealth of published thinking concerning 3) "family dynamics." This includes the well-read popular writings of
the social psychologists who deal with the individual,
given the family, and those who deal psychologically only
with the individual. On a popular level, little is understood about the dynamics of family and society.

To reduce all three areas from the abstract level to
dimensions that are workable, understandable, and therefore
useful for policy considerations, the following paper
presents a review of commonly used family models. In so
doing, a definition which is gaining more and more acceptance offers a starting point. "Any group of two or more
persons with a legal or biological relationship" (one of
several definitions employed by the Family Impact Seminar
of George Washington University) is a good attempt to
broaden the scope to include ties between people who do
not live together, and to account for the various "stages"
of families and their living arrangements. However, it
still fails to capture the essence of people grouping

themselves into families, and runs the risk of generating
a superficial analysis.

Ultimately, I believe that the realities of making policy
and the current stage of our social evolution argue for an
even broader, and more innovative concept of the family.
By accounting for the observed and logical variations in
family forms, this notion would provide a more accurate
picture of family connected with society and economy. It
should thereby permit more meaningful forecasts of the outcomes of a variety of policy choices and implications. This
conclusion derives from an examination of the several definitions currently employed by our society. The following
discussion covers the most widely recognized concepts of
family that produce definitions or models. Following each
model, a working definition is offered, along with an
analysis of its viability as a tool for social policy
decisions, and a comment on the political implications
of using each definition.

The Legalistic Model

Concept. The lowest common denominator of social order,
above the tribal level, is the law. Within the family
domain, the law, in its arbitrary and practical ways, provides a measure of homogeneity and makes society flow more
smoothly. In America, there is a relatively high degree
of voluntary acceptance of the law, since Americans expect
our laws to reflect our values. Although we in the United
States pride ourselves on the timeliness of our laws,
traditional English common law still largely shapes our
notions of what is "legitimate" in marriage and family
relationships. Legal restrictions assuring heterosexuality,
non-incestuous relationships, sexual access to one's mate,
and in some cases, laws which prohibit interracial and even
interreligious marriages are examples of the government's
"say-so" over family life decisions. As these legal definitions tend to dominate popular exposure, people believe
these laws to be derived from the "natural" order of life,
and thus they are acted out by substantial segments of our
society.

Working Definition. The working definition of a "legal
family," then, is that which is set out by law. Though
family law varies from state to state, it is commonly held
to mean a group consisting of married heterosexuals and their
"legitimate children." (Although there is a "contract"
implied in the old English law which sets out a division of
labor between the man and the woman, state governments do
not ordinarily interfere with on-going marriages, once their

legality has been initially established. Additionally,
relationships which have not been legally ordained are
usually considered legal after a statutorially established
period of time, regardless of the couple's consent to it.)
Therefore, a working legal definition of the family is the
relationship set out by the law of each state and usually
indicates relationships which have been officially registered by the state. This definition is predominantly used
by lawyers in courts when families are in conflict.

Viability for Policy Implementation. Because the law is
continually tested and applied, it can claim the tightest and
most arbitrary concepts of all ways of thinking within the
society; therefore, a legalistic definition of the family
eases data gathering, allowing a legalistic definition to be
buttressed by statistics.

     An historical review of family law reveals the demands
on family life in our society as it was forming. Large,
extended families were necessary when Americans settled the
wilderness. These families (by law or by the implications
of its absence) were required to take care of their young,
their retarded, the paupers, the criminals, their senile --
to provide in essence, a multi-faceted, private social
support system. Today, a study of social welfare laws (e.g.,
the various sections of the Social Security Act of the New
Deal) will reveal its connection with the smaller nuclear
groups which are able to survive the pressures of an economy
that requires a high degree of mobility and allows unprece-
dented personal freedom. Legal history, in another example,
also reveals how family forms have been remolded, ensuring
monogamy for the preservation of private property through
inheritance laws.

     Sadly enough, an understanding of historical family
law and its applications will also clearly expose the
cultural lag between what is "officially sanctioned" and
what people actually do. Perhaps law, especially family
law, is by nature rooted in the past. For this reason
alone, the legal definition of family has little ability
to significantly enlighten us about either the present or
the future.

Political Implications. Policies which are predominantly
based upon legal definitions of the family run the risk of
misrepresenting the actual life experiences of the mainstream
of people in families. Therefore, legal definitions and the
policies they generate tend to operate conservatively, if
not regressively. For a less than superficial analysis, one
must also look at the interests which are reflected in the

law-making process to see that law is a strong and effective
social control force benefitting the status quo.

The Structural Model

Concept. Living patterns, because they are concrete, re-
curring, and common experiences, lend themselves particularly
well to statistical reduction. Family living patterns such
as household arrangement (organization by age and sex),
residence, and formal relations to the labor market, are
census-type variables whose collective centers are often projected as "natural" or "average" family forms. This definition of family, then, merely describes how the group of
adults and children are organized.

Working Definition. Although many possible definitions can
be used in the structural model, the most common "profile"
of the family comes from definitions and variables used by
the U.S. Census Bureau. Family is defined as "two or more
persons residing together who are related by blood, marriage,
or adoption." Household is defined as "all persons occupying
a housing unit," with various stipulations to further define
the housing unit (e.g., a housing unit must have separate
kitchen facilities and a separate entrance, etc.). Other
structural variables used in conjunction with gathering data
about family include questions regarding number of children,
their ages, education level of "family head," and gender of
the "head of household." Although the strict definition used
by the Census Bureau is, at its base, merely a legal one,
other predominantly structural variables are largely empha-
sized in the final analysis.

Thus, structural definitions will reflect a gamut --
from the properties used by the Census Bureau to such a broad
concept as "domestic unit," which is variously defined as:
"those individuals living in the same economic unit" (used by
the Family Impact Seminar in searching the Catalogue of
Federal Domestic Assistance); or "a relatively permanent ongoing primary relationship which involves at least one adult
and one child under 18" (Interagency Panels Information
System maintained by Social Research Group of George Washington University). Structural definitions of one sort or
another are usually employed by policy makers and public
researchers who are required to show statistical conclusions
or linkages.

Viability for Policy Implementation. The argument for any
structural definition resembles that of the legalistic one:
it is arbitrary and easy to mold around accumulated statistics. It is particularly appropriate for an industrialized

society, wherein economic and social decisions are made and
assessed at a far-removed level. Again, however, structural
"averages" often do not account for actual experiences of
large segments of American society; in addition, they fail to
capture the true essence of family life.

Political Implications. To the extent that the organization
of households has to be subjected to statistical analysis for
research and policy decisions, it often implies an "acceptable manner" in which to organize one's family. Further,
because structural definitions must serve statistical interests and not offend implied notions of morality, the
structural model often generates extremely biased measure-
ment, analysis and legislation. For example, Census Bureau
statistics insist upon a "head of household" concerning a
relationship that is increasingly viewed by Americans as a
partnership; the Congress creates different tax rates for
married and unmarried couples; and the AFDC penalizes the
family in which an "able-bodied male," when present, does not
function as the family breadwinner. These examples point up
the penalties to which people are subjected if they do not,
through choice or circumstance, conform to the demands of
structural research tools for use by policy makers. The most
salient exposure of such coerced morality based on legal,
biological and living pattern biases is presented by Carol
Stack (elsewhere in the volume), and others on the subject
of the black family, which these very biases historically
and currently define as "non-family."

The Normative or Moral Model

Concept. Family is a universal and fundamental cultural
expression, bound up in the questions of "life's meaning."
Ideology -- whether myth or policy, religious or political --
creates real-life belief systems which form expectations of
what a family should be. This can and often does become the
ideal by which people set their own family standards, to the
best of their ability given other real-life constraints.

Working Definition. As with the "nuclear family," assumptions as to what lifestyles should be undergird notions that
are readily accepted as definitions. Principally, the
"nuclear family" as an ideal model assumes the moral or
normative rightness of biological links, legal recognition
(the main components used by a host of public agencies), and
a patriarchal hierarchy within the family. An HEW Task
Force on the Family reveals in a preliminary paper that if
federal social policy reflected a "neutral" stance to family
forms (eschewing incentives or disincentives), that the
"naturally preferred family model" would probably emerge

naturally, and the paper goes on to predict that it is
suspected this model would be the "traditional two-parent
family." (Unpublished paper representing intradepartmental discussions, dated January 10, 1977).

Religious doctrines normally openly address the family
from this angle. Any professional who works in a religious-
based agency or who sees her or his role as promoting the
"public interest" through an encouragement of these ideas is
also regarded as operating from a normative model. Even
those professionals who claim to be "value-free" may be
relying in the main on normative assumptions which go unrecognized.

Viability for Policy Implementation. If ideology is in-
corporated into a model and then used to generate research
and therefore social policy, it will undoubtedly reflect a
smaller or larger degree of lag between the theoretical
model and actual lifestyles. The fact is, even given the
strong belief in the "rightness" of these types of models,
people's personal family experiences often fall far short of
their expectations, as our limited indicators demonstrate.

Are research (the scientific kind) and policy (the
progressive kind) best served by ideological models, or by
those which accurately describe how people live? Since
ideological models do serve to maintain myths and hopes to
which people can be persuaded to aspire, especially in
certain "Camelot" policy periods, this may indeed be the
purpose of such models. This cannot, however, be regarded
as scientific.

Political Implications. Perhaps the gravest social and
personal costs associated with policy based on notions of
morality is the social label of "dysfunctional," "aberrant,"
or "unhealthy" -- the labels given to those families and
individuals who do not reflect normative family patterns.
It follows that there is a great deal of "blaming the vic-
tim," both by the government agencies with power to make
such judgments and, in the case of individuals, by people
forever struggling to reconcile their "oughts" with their
"ams." Constant comparison of one's reality to such an
"ideal-sold-as-reality" results in preoccupation with one's
shortcomings and an undue indictment of one's family as
"inadequate." This, of course, encourages and insures an
expanded and perpetuated social rehabilitation and therapy
enterprise. Diagnostic labels of "family dysfunction" are
widely in use today and will always be a moral and political
issue fought through the entire social policy-making
process. We create "sick" people through "sick" families,

as diagnosed, prescribed to, and thereby reinforced through
social policy.

The Functional Model

Concept.   Scholarly thinking plainly acknowledges the
family's connections with society and seeks to show how the
institution serves society.   The so-called "functions" of
the family as an institution of society are embodied in a
wide-ranging definition to which several academic disciplines
contribute in a segmented manner.   The general agreement is
that there are four fundamental functions of the family: to
reproduce (birth) new societal members in an orderly way; to
physically protect and to socialize those new members into
useful, non-destructive roles; to control, yet allow sexual
expression; and to serve as an efficient economic production
unit by means of cooperation.   Of these four functions,
economic productivity, first, and socialization, second, are
the predominant links between family and society.

Traditionally, however, American sociologists have
increasingly concluded that industrialization has almost
totally converted the family from a unit of production to a
unit of consumption.   Whereas the agrarian family worked the
land together in obvious production, the industrialized
family sends one member out to the factory or office to
function as the sole "breadwinner;" thereby, these scholars
have reasoned, this separated the family from work and the
workers.   In determining that the family's main societal
link (other than socializing its members) is consumption,
traditional sociologists have promoted the concept of the
family as a rather passive group which comes together for
the reason of sharing its consumption -- both of life
chances and of material products.   Consumption becomes a
means to happiness.   Therefore, we began to focus on those
happiness variables -- emotional nurturing, belonging,
"irrational caring and commitment" -- that are often experienced in connection with consumption habits.   This, of
course, has given direct theoretical rise to the link
between sociology and psychology in the area of family and
has been very productive on a mid-level basis.

The HEW Task Force on the Family, mentioned above,
best exemplifies the use of this fragmented functional model
in its preliminary definition of the family: "without regard to the reason for formation or the form it takes, any
combination of individuals which combine in willingness to
meet each others' needs and provide mutual support emotionally and/or financially may meet the tests of a family."
This definition assumes the self-determination of family

and, at this point, does not address those family systems
that are not "willed" by the participants. An extension of
the above is offered: "Whether by blood, religious, or legal
contract or simply mutual consent, any individuals sharing
or choosing to share each other's lives and/or living space
for any emotional, economic, or social reasons" can be considered a family. Again, this is a commendable attempt to
take consideration of so-called "alternative family life-
styles" and dispense with value judgments. But again, has
it succeeded in capturing the antecedent reasons why family
is formed?

Working Definition. The social tasks required of a family
and outlined above define the family in the functional model
and become its social raison d'être. Presumably, then, any
group meeting these criteria (more or less) could be considered a "family." Attempts to capture this orientation
in a working definition, however, can prove to be little
improvement, if any, over the limitations it seeks to
criticize. Note, for example, the definition used by the
Vanier Institute of the Family in Ottawa, Canada. In trying
to provide a functional working definition that is progressive, the Institute defines the domestic sector of our
economy as: "the daily performance of those necessary and
desirable familial activities on which personal, economic,
and social well-being are grounded." There appears to be
no less than a quantum leap from this description to the
process of fitting people into the description.

Those professions which need to keep in mind the link
between family and society are presently the ones most apt
to rely on the functional model -- psychologists, family-
system-oriented physicians, therapists, economists, etc.
The problem is, however, that each profession tends to
segment the function which best fits its needs, and this
works to distort the entire link between family and society.

Viability for Policy Implementation. The functional model,
in its entirety, is very useful when one wants to study the
dynamics of the family by viewing it over time or from culture to culture. It is perhaps the only model which readily
exposes the full spectrum of changes in the family institution; because of this, it is the best available model for
informing social policy intervention.

On the other hand, on a close examination of the previously mentioned preoccupation with the family as a consumption unit, we must assess the usefulness of our view of
the family as the chief provider of emotional support in
constructing social policy. Certainly individuals derive

important psychological benefits directly from their family membership, but two policy oriented questions must now be posed: 1) Is this the only antecedent reason people come together in the particular ways they do? (In other words, does anything other than "fate," "romantic" or sexual feelings and emotional need bear on our decisions to marry and procreate?) It is widely accepted in sociology that there is a socio-economic "pool" of potential mates that is antecedent to one's "personal and free" choice; 2) What can social policy reasonably be expected to do at this level? Can policy make people love each other or does it seek, rather, to minimize stressful and harmful conditions and create supportive social conditions which help release people's natural nurturing capacities. For example, what was the impact of the "man in the house" disincentive on welfare mothers trying to create supportive relationships with potential husbands and fathers? Do residential re- quirements that eliminate homosexual or unmarried couples constrain their ability to emotionally care for each other? And if these policies "cost" groups of people in their attempts to provide emotional support for each other, should not we concern ourselves with these "costs?"

The functional model poses largely technical (or operational) problems when policy relies on patterns of numbers supplied through statistical reduction. In thinking about how government should relate to family, these con- ceptual aspects of the family can hardly be ignored. In the matter of technical application, however, many problems yet abound.

Political Implications. If accurate prediction and sup- portive social services are the objects of social policy, the functional model has great potential. It appears to keep ideological considerations to a minimum and allows a much broader inter-societal perspective of family dynamics, an increasingly necessary way of perceiving the universal institution of the family. However, it must be noted that the greater the holistic approach to the family, the more comprehensive social policy most become.

The Social Psychological Model

Concept. The way people behave and feel in their per- sonally experienced family life is a concern in promoting the well-being and happiness of individuals. Making functional adults out of children involves the process of socialization both from the developing child's perspective and from a parenting perspective. (In the case of childless- ness, the social psychological model is concerned with how adults engage in relationships with each other.) This perspective views the family as a fundamental social group which both acts upon the individual and is in turn acted upon by the individual (but it is basically devoid of treatment of any larger societal context).

Working Definition. A working definition of the family will revolve around the study of the individual in a group process, with emphasis on parents and children in their special patterns of interaction. This is most practically translated into the interaction among people (parents, children, and other adults) who live in the same residence and/or have significant and frequent contact. Social psychologists usually focus on the individual and her/his self-identified "significant others" as the definition of the family group, and they, along with therapists, and social welfare workers are almost required to work from this model.

Viability for Policy Implementation. This approach provides a more precise description of family behavior, inasmuch as it can be known to those who observe and analyze family life, which has tended to be very private in the U.S. Case studies, which have a particular depth of insight, offer the closest glimpse of real life family dynamics. If more than description is desired, however, and if a broader tool of explanation is needed to link family with society, then documenting patterns of family interaction is little more than journalism.

Political Implications. To the extent that social policy necessarily addresses the interface of family and other social institutions -- principally economic -- a knowledge of intrafamily behavior is limited in its benefits. That private area of people's lives, although surely affected by social policy, in the long run only remotely affects massive societal machinery. However, inasmuch as social policy must also be concerned with smaller units, especially when individuals themselves become problems for society, this aspect of family requires meaningful consideration. All broadly defined "therapy systems," especially the criminal justice system, must ultimately confront these family patterns of interaction.

A New Definition of Family

The Family Approaching 1980. As the economy continues to change, and systems of the world increasingly acknowledge

one another -- as recent years have shown -- the decidedly
moral and romantic notions of family are beginning to lose
their prominence. They give way to some fruitful, new modes
of inquiry. The question arises: Can we find a model which
will account for variety in family forms and also will capture family life's raison d'être?

With full deference given to all other functions of
the family, it is the necessity to cooperate through the
family for survival and mutual benefit that appears to offer
the best connection between individuals in their families
and individuals in their society.

Most important, the family as a unit of economic production is a group which is daily about the business of
converting the abilities of its members into resources for
the collective, long-term sustenance of the group. Work,
in both its social and economic sense, cannot be separated
from family. Work must come to be officially recognized
as encompassing far more than mere wage labor. Today's
policy makers tred -- or are nudged -- in this area of work
and family; and in a very real sense, families will not
begin to meet people's needs until we recognize that what
people do with the hours of their day not only make them
societal members -- citizens, if you will -- but developed
human beings who become more or less able to sustain themselves. Children, therefore, work when they go to school.
Homemakers work when they maintain an environment that nur-
tures and produces work energy and potential. The unemployed
work when they "hustle" to insure their daily existence.
[It is interesting to note that some elderly make up a group
that does not fit this model. Retired senior citizens on
public or private pensions can be considered workers within
this new perception if they: a) physically take care of
themselves, b) provide care for members of their extended
families, and/or c) do volunteer/civic work. However, the
institutionalized elderly or those totally and physically
dependent on their families are like helpless children in
that they are mainly "acted upon" in this society. Not being
able even to maintain themselves, these groups would not
readily fit into this model. A further analysis along this
line might be helpful in the much needed breakthrough on
theory of the elderly in the U.S. society.]

Family and Work

Concept. The family is the smallest group of individuals
whose mutual need is to survive. They survive through production. Production, then, is one's work, waged or not,

exchanged or not. Work, in this context, becomes that use of the hours of the day which directly or indirectly contributes to the family's present or future survival. Under this definition, people are necessarily engaged in work most of their days, most of their lives.

Working Definition. At this stage, there are certain problems in translating this way of perceiving the family's social and economic rationale into a working definition that will allow computers and statisticians to formulate tidy graphs and charts. However, let us initially propose that the family is a group of people who are bound by their common work efforts, from which their common consumption derives. This definition will necessarily give each "family member" her or his proper recognition in the process of family interaction with society, and will not exclude family forms of any type.

Viability for Policy Implementation. One of the biggest drawbacks to advocating a new conceptualization of family is in getting respondents to perceive in new ways so that the research process can be valid. To throw off the legal and biological and residential restrictions could cause confusion on the part of both investigators and respondents. It would certainly make the "head of household" concept passé. It would bring into full focus the unrecognized labor of the homemaker. It would lift students out of the "unemployed ghetto" to which they are accustomed. It would expose publicly the real results of inadequate welfare measures. It also brings into sharper focus the actual work habits of families and the variation in their values.

A producer-consumer model would comfortably take into account all forms of family life, conventional or not. It would also assure that families will not become isolated groups with no discernable connection to society. It would easily and appropriately monitor changes in both values and social conditions. For these reasons, this type of definition, when more fully developed (i.e., its measurable dimensions identified), should be better able to explain and to predict the dynamics of family and society. It is not easily reducible to numbers and might require methodologies that are not as "acceptable" as survey research. It will also severely question the status quo notion of the family as "sacred."

Political Implications. There are a host of political implications to the adoption of a producer-consumer concept of family, many of which are not even perceptible at this time. For one thing, the male breadwinner model would be

rendered virtually meaningless. Therefore, the attempt to
push the working woman into that same model would also lead
nowhere. Our previous ability to separate work from family
will fail. The previous ability to separate children and
their care from working parents will fail. Workers would be
seen as family members with constant, on-going responsibilities, and family members would, by definition, come to
consider themselves in the light of their total work.
Established moral forces will find their proclamation of
personal life complicated by economic and political dragons.
And the gap between what we wish our policies to achieve and
what they actually do will be exposed. The inherent alien-
ation in an artificial separation of family and society, of
our personal life from our societal life, will be reduced
as people come to see themselves as performing simultaneous
roles, and as social policy begins to better meet people's
needs.

References

1. Women's Washington Representative (June 12, 1977),
    p. 3.

3

The Household School as Life-Span Learning Center

Winifred I. Warnat

It is generally assumed that our formal education institutions--public and private; elementary, secondary, and higher education--bear the predominant responsibility for, and conduct most of the activities pertinent to individual learning in our society. Not only have we assigned to the formal education institutions the vast bulk of our society's cognitive learning with its concentration on knowledge acquisition and skills development, we have also added to the responsibilities of formal education in recent years. Further confusing its role and function in relation to individual learning is our increasing assumption that formal education institutions also encompass personal learning in the affective domain. But even as we have directed greater and greater portions of our public attention and resources toward our formal education institutions, the informal education institution--the household school--in fact, has remained the basis of affective learning. Yet to be acknowledged and utilized by public policy, this most vital education institution has as its nucleus the family.

Formal education has become a monolithic structure of such proportions that it has assumed or has been assigned functions which it has virtually no capacity to perform. To date, the adversary relationship between formal education and the family continues to strengthen. The family has yet to be acknowledged as the foundation for individual learning. Rather than being perceived and used as a primary resource, the family is viewed by the education monolith in a "patient-doctor" perspective--constantly ailing and in need of assistance. This is a perspective shared with and reinforced by the other formal social service institutions. It is obvious that this erroneous perspective needs to be corrected, and that the relationship which currently exists between formal education and the family needs to undergo dramatic change. An initial step in doing so is the identification and examination of <u>the household school as life-span learning center</u>.

Household School Defined

As has been previously mentioned, the core of the household school is the family, inclusive of all variations thereof. The household school encompasses all family members and addresses all roles played by each member within and without the family construct. In this context, each member, at various points in time, functions as both learner and educator throughout his life span. From the time of his birth and until his death, every human being is a member of a household school. While the family structure varies, even those who live alone have membership in a household school. In their alternative household, family membership may instead consist of friends, neighbors, or co-workers.

The family structure provides the basic environment in which the household school operates. In the context of the household school, the environment encompasses the conditions, including social and cultural circumstances, which directly influence the family structure, and the specific, individual membership of that family structure. Within this environment, affective learning occurs which concentrates on individuality and the socialization process. Affective learning in this context addresses the life roles a person plays, the feelings he has, the values and beliefs he espouses, and the behaviors he expresses. The environment in which the household school functions, be it a nuclear, extended, single-parent, reconstituted, kin network, or commune family, is a major determinant influencing a person's affective learning capacity and functioning.

Life-span learning is the primary function of the household school. It encompasses a person's response and adaptation to his evolving life experience with its critical incidents* and transition times**. This function involves four major tasks which serve to develop each family member's awareness and understanding, coping capacity, and ability to adapt to change. These tasks are:

---

*<u>critical incident</u>--a significant event such as marriage, death of a loved one, divorce, retirement, in a person's life which has inordinate impact on his life process.
**<u>transition time</u>--the adjustment period preceding and/or following the occurrence of a critical incident.

1. <u>Role Selection</u> - the identification, preparation for and performance of the various life roles performed by each family member throughout his life span;

2. <u>Personality Acquisition</u> - the recognition and expression of personal feelings concerning one's self and his relationship to others;

3. <u>Value Formation</u> - the realization of and adherence to the values and beliefs endorsed by the household school membership;

4. <u>Behavioral Patterning</u> - the acknowledgement and implementation of individual behaviors conditioned by interaction with the household school environment.

<u>The mission of the household school is to nurture and cultivate the individuality and socialization of each family member through the learning process</u>.

A Collective Management System

In essence, the household school represents a collective management system, which operates on an experientially-based learning mode to improve the affective functioning of the individual, both inside and outside of his family environment. In this learning mode, family members are continuously experiencing or living through a sequence of five steps through which the tasks of the household school are accomplished. These steps are:

(1) the <u>identification</u> of roles, feelings, values and beliefs, and behaviors practiced by the household members;

(2) based on the identification, <u>selections</u> are made of those roles, feelings, values and beliefs, and behaviors that appear appropriate and/or compatible for ones self;

(3) after the selection, <u>performance</u> of those choices occurs;

(4) given the initial performances, <u>modification</u> is made based on feedback from household members and others, which accommodates how the family member perceives himself, as well as how he interprets how others perceive him;

(5) once all this has been processed, the <u>adoption</u> of the chosen and rehearsed performances pertaining to the roles, feelings, behaviors, values and beliefs, take place to form the compatible configuration of the family member's own <u>personal management system</u>.

Life-Span Learning Curriculum

Learning activites conducted within the hypothetical construct of the household school concentrate on the life span
learning curriculum. The curriculum addresses the four tasks
of the household school by focusing on the critical incidents
and transition times within the life experience of each family member. Informal and structured in design, the life
span learning curriculum is geared to respond to the constantly evolving critical incidents and transition times as
they are experienced by each family member. The curriculum
as presented here, encompasses four content areas based on
the four tasks of the household school. Related to the affective domain, they are: (1) Role Selection, (2) Personality
Acquisition, (3) Value Formation, and (4) Behavioral Patterning. Learning activities conducted in the household school
concentrate essentially on two approaches--observation and
experience, which include the modeling of specific role-
related behaviors. These activities also represent the five
functions performed by each household member as he responds
to a critical incident.

In order to better understand the household school as life
span learning center and the resultant personal management
system, four examples are presented which apply the five se-
quential steps identified above. These examples are based on
four critical incidents occurring within the context of the
content areas of the life span learning curriculum. Even
though all four content areas of the curriculum normally
operate simultaneously in terms of such critical incidents
and their related transition times, the examples used here
will concentrate on only <u>one</u> dimension of each for the purpose of illustration. They are discussed accordingly:

Examples

Content Area		Critical Incident
I-A. Role Selection	I-B.	Birth of First Child
II-A. Personality Acquisition	II-B.	Death of Loved One
III-A. Value Formation	III-B.	Divorce
IV-A. Behavioral Patterning	IV-B.	Retirement

   I-A. Role Selection - Every person assumes many roles
throughout his lifetime, which encompass different sets of
expectations, responsibilities, skills, and behaviors. Some
of the roles a person fills include being a man/woman, a sib-
ling, a parent, a spouse, a single; being a friend, a lover, a

neighbor; being a student, a teacher, a worker, etc. The individual must be prepared to perform in a number of roles at
any given time, frequently requiring the ability to make
rapid changes in sentiment and behavior to accommodate the
demands of each role.

It is a major task of the household school to prepare its
members for the various role functions each will encounter.
Preconceived notions of how each role is to be satisfied are
evident within the family membership, both in the form of
role models and didactic instruction. The household school
further reinforces this instruction by providing (1) recognition of given role expectations, (2) observation of others
in the various roles, and (3) motivation to function in the
prescribed and accepted mode. Feedback is a constant dynamic of the household school with most household members assessing the appropriateness of given role performances and responding to them accordingly.

Whether one is functioning in the role of parent, student, or
worker, certain performance characteristics are cultivated
within the household school. Most often, the parent or
parent surrogate serves as the educator in teaching the dynamics of task completion, orderliness, punctuality, performance, and aspiration level--dynamics pertinent to all three
roles. The educators in the household school provide role
models for the learner through their performance and response
to the expectations of various roles. The type of inducement
provided the learner for mastering the dynamics mentioned
will also influence the effectiveness of the household school
educator.

I-B. Birth of First Child. The transition time associated with the birth of a child includes a preparation period
during which the upcoming, new role of parent, as well as the
rearrangement of existing roles, is explored. The identification of various parental responsibilities and role-related
behaviors occurs. The most influential input by the household school membership for this critical incident is normally
provided by the parents of the parents-to-be. However,
friends, neighbors, and siblings may also provide parent
models of child rearing. We learn most about the parent role
from our own parents throughout our own growing up period.
The years of exposure to various role models is the most
important input to adopting the role, rather than that of
the nine month gestation period. This input is crystal-
lized when we are called upon to occupy the role of parent.
A selection process then occurs in which the new parent
behaviors are assumed and accommodations to existing roles
are made.

When the infant actually arrives, the preparation period ends with the parents beginning their performance in their new role. The new parents assay behaviors which seem most suitable, based upon the role models which have been provided them by the "faculty" of the household school. As the new parents test their behaviors and adjust other role-related behaviors, modification is made in the performance of the new parent role, in terms of: (1) acknowledged expectations involved with performing in the new role; (2) concentration on the parent role performances best suited to the character of the newly-emerging family; and (3) acceptance and continued refinement of the evolving parent role. Finally, the adoption of the parent role occurs as judgements are made establishing its design and continuity over time through trial and error experience, and through feedback consultation with other members of the household school.

II-A. Personality Acquisition. Life encompasses a broad range of emotional stimuli, which elicit differing responses. Within any twenty-four hour period, an individual may experience numerous changes in feelings, which may include love, fear, joy, boredom, excitement, sorrow, anger, nervousness, and mellowness, etc. The individual's expression of those feelings in turn impacts upon relationships with others, constantly requiring him/her to make adjustments to his/her feeling state in terms of both his/her personal and social milieu. How a person adjusts is significantly influenced by the family environment.

In terms of feelings, the second task of the household school --acquisition of personality--concentrates on both the individual and the social dynamics of each family member. It focuses on assisting each member in developing an awareness of his personal feelings as they surface. Then, based on the determination of their appropriateness made by the household membership, the member adjusts their manifestations. Expressions of and responses to the range of emotions are experientially defined and demonstrated by each household member, which in turn, provides the feeling modality endorsed by the household school.

Each household member serves as educator in the household school, because each provides an example of feelings and related expressive behaviors. Using this as the data base, the learner in the household school has an entire repertoire of expressions to use concerning his feelings. Depending upon the family environment, he may either accept or reject choices from the available examples. If he selects from those available, it is likely that he will emulate with modification the expression of those feelings to which he is most frequently exposed, if not those deemed most appropriate.

II-B. Death of a Loved One. In the critical incident
of the death of a loved one, only when death is anticipated
due to illness is there a preparation period in the transition
time. Once death is seen as inevitable by the household members, they begin to make an accommodation to this impending
reality. In this incident, the identification of one's own
specific feelings is often difficult because of the intense
feelings expressed by other mourning household members at
both an overt and covert level. The subconscious selection
of feelings which serve to perpetuate a new and hopefully
desired way of life is complicated by the sense of loss and
the realization of dramatic adjustments to the continuation
of life. The new way of life may manifest itself in a performance which may capitalize on the altered situation, or
be characterized by inconsolable grief, fear of living, or
a newly-found mellowness. Throughout the transition time,
adjustment of feelings pertinent to the loss are made.
Modification of the new way of life is accompanied by an
entrenchment of emotions based on past reminiscence and
future anticipation of the unknown. The sensitizing which
occurs contributes to a peaking in certain emotions and a
numbing of others, as adoption to the new way of life occurs.

III-A. Value Formation. Inherent to all families is a
system of values and beliefs. This system not only provides
the individual with the basic criteria for determining good
from bad, right from wrong, and truth from untruth; it
also provides the maturing household members with their first
over-all explanation of reality in terms of how and why the
world society and its institutions work the way they do.
Based on the definitive interpretations and rationales provided, each family member is expected to more or less adhere
to the identified values and beliefs.

A crucial aspect of the third major task of the household
school--value formation--is to continuously reinforce the
system of beliefs and values espoused by the household membership. This is accomplished by clearly identifying what
those values and beliefs are, and by providing support for
their enforcement. Because of their abstract nature, the
interpretations given by the household members are crucial
in the enforcement process. It becomes the responsibility of
the household school to develop an awareness of the impact of
deviation from the approved values and beliefs. In an effort
to renew the compliance of a household member who disavows
them, the household membership may assume either a judgemen-
tal perspective in which such deviation results in some form
of punishment for the erring family member, or a forgiveness
perspective in which the deviation results in absolution.
Often, of course, the household employs both.

Explicit explanations pertinent to the approved system of
values and beliefs in the household school are mandatory for
implementation. Those household members most responsible for
decision-making within the family serve as the values educators in the household school. The learner internalizes his
endorsement of the selected values and beliefs based on the
consistency and frequency of their verbal judication, and on
their observable portrayal through the acting out of family
members. Rejection of values and beliefs by the learner
often results in either voluntary withdrawal from or ostra-
cism by the family.

III-B. Divorce. In terms of life events, perhaps noth-
ing challenges personal values and beliefs more than the critical incident of divorce. The preparation period encompasses
the waning marriage time once the possiblity of divorce has
been consciously contemplated, as well as the period of formal
separation. When the divorce occurs, the transition time
involves the actualizing and operating of the newly determined life style. The identification function is certainly
complex, as previous values concerning family, children, and
social acceptance must all be re-weighed as a new family
structure, still part of the household school, is created.
In addition, the spiritual foundation is also questioned as
one reorders his values and beliefs, which now may be in conflict with his religious affiliation. To accommodate the
adjustment to a different living arrangement, this reordering
involves a critical selection process. As the adjustment is
made, various levels of performance are tried and tested to
re-assess and re-establish a personal sense of values and
beliefs. As this occurs, modification is made which serves
to clarify and solidify those chosen. Finally, adoption
occurs as the divorced individuals integrate into day-to-day
life as unmarried persons with altered perceptions, responsibilities, and behaviors grounded in the tested and modified
values and beliefs. As a new component of the extended household with its re-arranged membership, divorced individuals
may form a new household, or reintegrate with those of their
respective parents.

IV-A. Behavioral Patterning. The dominant, fundamental
influence of the family--through the household school--in
determining individual behavior patterns is well established.
The determination of appropriate and inappropriate behaviors is inherent to the household environment and daily life
therein. The patterns of behavior which one learns and uses
in such an environment are conditioned by the models presented
by family members in terms of their own actions and reactions
to given circumstances and emotions.

Bibliography

Barron, W. E. and Charles R. Kelso. "Adult Functional Competency: A Summary." Unpublished Report, University [of] Texas, Study for the U.S. Office of Education, March [1976].

Bettleheim, Bruno. "Some Tentative Remarks on the Problems of the Family," Center dialogue, Chicago: The Center for the Study of Democratic Institutions, University of Chicago, May 13, 1976. Unpublished manuscript.

Bishof, Ledford J. *Adult Psychology*, 2 ed., New York: Harper and Row, 1976.

Carter, Hugh and Paul C. Glick. *Marriage and Divorce: A Social and Economic Study*, 2 ed., Cambridge, Mass: Harvard University Press, 1976.

Downey, Constance, et.al. *Family Impact Task Force Report*. Office of Special Concerns, U.S. Department of Health, Education and Welfare, January 10, 1977. Unpublished manuscript.

Kimmel, Douglas C. *Adulthood and Aging*, New York: John Wiley and Sons, 1974.

Neugarten, Bernice L. *Middle Age and Aging*, Chicago: University of Chicago Press, 1968.

Otto, Herbert A. (Ed.). *The Family in Search of a Future*, New York: Appleton Century Crofts, 1970

Schulz, David A. The Changing Family: Its Function and Future, 2 ed., Englewood Cliffs, N.J.: Prentice Hall, 1976.

U.S. Department of Commerce. *Social Indicators, 1976*, Washington, D.C.: U.S. Government Printing Office, December, 1977.

Vaughn, V.C., and T.B. Brazelton (Eds.). *The Family--Can it Be Saved?* Chicago: Year Book Medical Publishers, 1976.

In its fourth major task, the household school serves to mold the behavior patterns of the individual to accommodate society, as modeled by family. This is achieved by the individual's (1) observation of the behavior of household members, (2) emulation of the observed behaviors, and (3) testing of alternative behaviors for acceptance or rejection by the household membership. A crucial function of the household school, as it molds the behavior of each member, is determining the spectrum of allowable behaviors, and the reinforcement of those which are most effective.

IV-B. Retirement. Even though the concept of retirement is contemplated for some time prior to its actual occurrance, the preparation period of the transition time is nominal at best. As with other major alterations in an individual's social or economic status, the realization of retirement's total range of implications is generally not evident until it is an accomplished fact. The identification task here concentrates on determining new behaviors relative to unallocated time, the reduction of work life, and the increase in family and leisure life. How to adjust established living patterns to the now more abundant discretionary time, reduced income, and altered family structure involves an exacting selection process. As one selects new behaviors and attempts to change old ones, the performance function places emphasis on using time differently, which serves to establish a new and rearranged pattern of living. Behaviors reflect revised perceptions of personal worth, new dependencies and independences, and changed role-functions in the established family structure. Modification of behavior occurs through relationships with family members and the incremental establishment of a social environment conducive to the new life-style. In terms of the household school, adoption is facilitated largely by the responsiveness of the household membership to the various dimensions of the changed life pattern.

Public Policy Implications of the Household School

The family or primary group, which stands at the center of an ever-extending network of human relationships for most people, also stands at the center of a life-span learning process for most individuals. The principal context of this life-span learning process is the household school; that is, the family as it interacts physically and emotionally with the immediate community and the larger world. In its day-to-day interpretations of its environment and rationalization of its collective mutual behaviors, the household school provides both the content and context for most of the affective learning of its members, with particular impact during childhood, and later,

during the critical incidents of adult life. Through the
mechanisms of mutual, interactive role-modeling, involving
the unique dynamics of each person who contributes to the life-
span learning curriculum, the household school provides each
member with the skills to manage the affective dimensions of
his or her life--a personal life management system. This
life management system includes our basic understanding of
how and why society and its institutions behave the way they
do. It includes our comprehension of human nature, our sen-
sitivity to personal/individual differences among people,
and our need to accommodate to others in order to function
effectively in our various life roles, e.g., worker, parent,
consumer, spouse, supervisor, etc. Finally, the household
school helps its members to establish sound behavior patterns
and communications skills to further promote effective inter-
personal relations.

In sum, the household school concept represents one of a number of ways in which to functionally define the family. It
is not a new perception, although as presented in the preceeding pages, the household school concept represents a more
comprehensive development of the perception than has been
previously advanced. Clearly, we have long understood and
accepted the fact that human development is, first and fore-
most, dependent upon one's experience in his or her early
primary group environment. By logical extension, the family
or other primary group--operating as a household school--
remains a significant force for shaping the individual
throughout his or her life span, and this is likely to be so
regardless of the family's structure or modus vivendi.

Accepting these perceptions, what implications does the household school concept contain for public policy toward the
family? Elsewhere in this volume, David Snyder observes that,
while the basic data make it clear that the family is both
individually and collectively, a powerful, productive economic unit in our society, no public policy or program perceives of or deals with the family in this light. Similarly,
the household school concept reveals the family as the primary institution in our society for providing learning in the
affective domain with major influence on the cognitive domain
as well. Yet, it is not viewed as a potential resource or
ally by any of the public agencies or programs with concerns
for the functional capacity or performance of the individual
in our society.

A principal reason for this discontinuity between social
function and public policy is the fact that there is extremely
limited scholarly knowledge concerning the affective dimensions of learning. As a result, we have tended to deprecate

the significance of the family's contributions to so
this regard. In a nation where research suggests th
of the adult population may be functionally incompet
cope with commonplace, everyday tasks, (Barron & Kel
would appear to be folly for public education to col
ignoring the household school. Public policy must
view the family and other primary groups as educati
institutions which contribute uniquely and signific
individual learning and development.

Specifically, this means that a national education
the family must be developed which builds upon the
inherent to the primary group--regardless of its fo
which supports rather than supplants family functic
such a policy, the formal education institutions at
should collaborate with families on a collegial bas
cultivating both the cognitive and affective learni
ties and performances of family members throughout
lives. Through the specific programs of this educa
policy, families should be provided with the resou
the opportunities to maximize their capabilities fo
ing the performance of their members as contributo
larger community. The ultimate goal of such a pol
be to assure the role of the household school as a
independent agency for stimulating and facilitatin
ate social change within the context of a stronger
broadly defined family institution for the post-in
society.

Extended Familial Networks

An Emerging Model for the
21st Century Family

Carol B. Stack

Introduction

Poor people have lots of relatives. Their families are large, and they tend to live relatively near one another. In contemporary industrial society, ties of kinship promote the daily survival of poor whites, blacks, chicanos, and orientals. Yet, many social scientists assert that the small, "nuclear" family of a husband, wife and their children is ideally adapted to the requirements of industrial society.

Historians of the family are in fact currently debating the impact of industrialism on the family, the importance of kinship in the last two hundred years, and changes in the quality of personal life. This scholarly attention reflects the growing public concern over recent changes in the size and structure of the modern family. Each new set of statistics on working mothers, on the rates of marriage, birth, and divorce, and on single-parent and single-person households creates great alarm.

In America today, the middle classes are clearly re-structuring their family life. Thus, experts say they are concerned about the "future of the family." Most books and articles on the topic, whether from the academic press or the popular press or the media, tend to focus on the trends and pressures affecting the middle classes, and on the future of the idealized nuclear family. Very few articles deal with poor people of the future. Similarly, in discussions on the history of the family, many historians have accepted the primacy of the idealized nuclear family. Those few who speculate on the future of the family have also been generally inclined to limit their predictions to changes occurring in the family life of the middle classes. Their scenarios reflect the future of families like "The

Jetsons," the television cartoon characters whose suburban
life style is already geared (or rather, wired), to the
space age.

The purpose of this paper is to compare the future of
the poor and of the more affluent middle-class families, in
light of the ways they have coped with industrial capitalism
in the past. We will review the emergence of the nuclear
family, and the extent to which the middle-class model has
been the sole basis for predictions of change in the American family. Likewise we will preview the yet unwritten
history of the lower-class family and its probable future.

To a great extent, middle-class families are currently
being confronted with problems similar to those faced by
poor families in the past and present. It is the central
thesis of this paper that the ability of poor families to
cope with economic exigencies (e.g., recurrent unemployment,
the need for a mother's wage, etc.), to build cooperative
networks, and to transcend biology in building intimate
relationships (Kanter) can teach us a great deal about the
future of the American family in general, and the shaping
of public policies affecting the family.

Recently, Kenneth Keniston, Executive Director of the
Carnegie Council on Children, and a well-known expert on
family and child welfare policy, wrote an article in the New
York Times entitled, "The Emptying Family." (1) In this
article, Keniston argues that the exaltation of children
and the prolonged retention of children within the nuclear
family--values which he believes to be characteristic to
American society--are in a state of decline. Keniston fears
that the modern middle-class family is emptying out--
actually losing its members. He sees that fewer people
than ever are at home to raise children, that "more than
half of school-age children now have mothers who work outside the home, mostly full time." He concludes that women's
work is associated with divorce, and has caused parents to
rear children without spouses. Ultimately, Keniston equates
the rising employment of women outside the home, and divorce,
with the destruction of the family.

The family of reference here is, of course, the nuclear
family--the intense, introspective, privatized family of
Freud, God-given, natural unit of society which is charged
to cradle the search for happiness amidst the perils of the
industrial bureaucratic metropolis. And, Keniston's primary concern is the structural change occurring within the
American family that leaves fewer people at home to raise
children.

In its fourth major task, the household school serves to mold the behavior patterns of the individual to accommodate society, as modeled by family. This is achieved by the individual's (1) observation of the behavior of household members, (2) emulation of the observed behaviors, and (3) testing of alternative behaviors for acceptance or rejection by the household membership. A crucial function of the household school, as it molds the behavior of each member, is determining the spectrum of allowable behaviors, and the reinforcement of those which are most effective.

IV-B. Retirement. Even though the concept of retirement is contemplated for some time prior to its actual occurance, the preparation period of the transition time is nominal at best. As with other major alterations in an individual's social or economic status, the realization of retirement's total range of implications is generally not evident until it is an accomplished fact. The identification task here concentrates on determining new behaviors relative to unallocated time, the reduction of work life, and the increase in family and leisure life. How to adjust established living patterns to the now more abundant discretionary time, reduced income, and altered family structure involves an exacting selection process. As one selects new behaviors and attempts to change old ones, the performance function places emphasis on using time differently, which serves to establish a new and rearranged pattern of living. Behaviors reflect revised perceptions of personal worth,new dependencies and independences, and changed role-functions in the established family structure. Modification of behavior occurs through relationships with family members and the incremental establishment of a social environment conducive to the new life-style. In terms of the household school, adoption is facilitated largely by the responsiveness of the household membership to the various dimensions of the changed life pattern.

Public Policy Implications of the Household School

The family or primary group, which stands at the center of an ever-extending network of human relationships for most people, also stands at the center of a life-span learning process for most individuals. The principal context of this life-span learning process is the household school; that is, the family as it interacts physically and emotionally with the immediate community and the larger world. In its day-to-day interpretations of its environment and rationalization of its collective mutual behaviors, the household school provides both the content and context for most of the affective learning of its members, with particular impact during childhood, and later,

during the critical incidents of adult life. Through the
mechanisms of mutual, interactive role-modeling, involving
the unique dynamics of each person who contributes to the life-
span learning curriculum, the household school provides each
member with the skills to manage the affective dimensions of
his or her life--a personal life management system. This
life management system includes our basic understanding of
how and why society and its institutions behave the way they
do. It includes our comprehension of human nature, our sen-
sitivity to personal/individual differences among people,
and our need to accommodate to others in order to function
effectively in our various life roles, e.g., worker, parent,
consumer, spouse, supervisor, etc. Finally, the household
school helps its members to establish sound behavior patterns
and communications skills to further promote effective inter-
personal relations.

In sum, the household school concept represents one of a number of ways in which to functionally define the family. It
is not a new perception, although as presented in the preceeding pages, the household school concept represents a more
comprehensive development of the perception than has been
previously advanced. Clearly, we have long understood and
accepted the fact that human development is, first and fore-
most, dependent upon one's experience in his or her early
primary group environment. By logical extension, the family
or other primary group--operating as a household school--
remains a significant force for shaping the individual
throughout his or her life span, and this is likely to be so
regardless of the family's structure or modus vivendi.

Accepting these perceptions, what implications does the household school concept contain for public policy toward the
family? Elsewhere in this volume, David Snyder observes that,
while the basic data make it clear that the family is both
individually and collectively, a powerful, productive economic unit in our society, no public policy or program perceives of or deals with the family in this light. Similarly,
the household school concept reveals the family as the primary institution in our society for providing learning in the
affective domain with major influence on the cognitive domain
as well. Yet, it is not viewed as a potential resource or
ally by any of the public agencies or programs with concerns
for the functional capacity or performance of the individual
in our society.

A principal reason for this discontinuity between social
function and public policy is the fact that there is extremely
limited scholarly knowledge concerning the affective dimensions of learning. As a result, we have tended to deprecate

the significance of the family's contributions to society in this regard. In a nation where research suggests that 15-25% of the adult population may be functionally incompetent to cope with commonplace, everyday tasks, (Barron & Kelso), it would appear to be folly for public education to continue ignoring the household school. Public policy must come to view the family and other primary groups as educational institutions which contribute uniquely and significantly to individual learning and development.

Specifically, this means that a national education policy on the family must be developed which builds upon the strengths inherent to the primary group--regardless of its form--and which supports rather than supplants family functions. Under such a policy, the formal education institutions at all levels should collaborate with families on a collegial basis in cultivating both the cognitive and affective learning capacities and performances of family members throughout their lives. Through the specific programs of this educational policy, families should be provided with the resources and the opportunities to maximize their capabilities for supporting the performance of their members as contributors to the larger community. The ultimate goal of such a policy would be to assure the role of the household school as an effective, independent agency for stimulating and facilitating appropriate social change within the context of a stronger, more broadly defined family institution for the post-industrial society.

Bibliography

Barron, W. E. and Charles R. Kelso. "Adult Functional Competency: A Summary." Unpublished Report, University of Texas, Study for the U.S. Office of Education, March 1975.

Bettleheim, Bruno. "Some Tentative Remarks on the Problems of the Family," Center dialogue, Chicago: The Center for the Study of Democratic Institutions, University of Chicago, May 13, 1976. Unpublished manuscript.

Bishof, Ledford J. *Adult Psychology*, 2 ed., New York: Harper and Row, 1976.

Carter, Hugh and Paul C. Glick. *Marriage and Divorce: A Social and Economic Study*, 2 ed., Cambridge, Mass: Harvard University Press, 1976.

Downey, Constance, et.al. *Family Impact Task Force Report*. Office of Special Concerns, U.S. Department of Health, Education and Welfare, January 10, 1977. Unpublished manuscript.

Kimmel, Douglas C. *Adulthood and Aging*, New York: John Wiley and Sons, 1974.

Neugarten, Bernice L. *Middle Age and Aging*, Chicago: University of Chicago Press, 1968.

Otto, Herbert A. (Ed.). *The Family in Search of a Future*, New York: Appleton Century Crofts, 1970

Schulz, David A. The Changing Family: Its Function and Future, 2 ed., Englewood Cliffs, N.J.: Prentice Hall, 1976.

U.S. Department of Commerce. *Social Indicators, 1976*, Washington, D.C.: U.S. Government Printing Office, December, 1977.

Vaughn, V.C., and T.B. Brazelton (Eds.). *The Family—Can it Be Saved?* Chicago: Year Book Medical Publishers, 1976.

Extended Familial Networks

An Emerging Model for the 21st Century Family

Carol B. Stack

Introduction

Poor people have lots of relatives. Their families are large, and they tend to live relatively near one another. In contemporary industrial society, ties of kinship promote the daily survival of poor whites, blacks, chicanos, and orientals. Yet, many social scientists assert that the small, "nuclear" family of a husband, wife and their children is ideally adapted to the requirements of industrial society.

Historians of the family are in fact currently debating the impact of industrialism on the family, the importance of kinship in the last two hundred years, and changes in the quality of personal life. This scholarly attention reflects the growing public concern over recent changes in the size and structure of the modern family. Each new set of statistics on working mothers, on the rates of marriage, birth, and divorce, and on single-parent and single-person households creates great alarm.

In America today, the middle classes are clearly re-structuring their family life. Thus, experts say they are concerned about the "future of the family." Most books and articles on the topic, whether from the academic press or the popular press or the media, tend to focus on the trends and pressures affecting the middle classes, and on the future of the idealized nuclear family. Very few articles deal with poor people of the future. Similarly, in discussions on the history of the family, many historians have accepted the primacy of the idealized nuclear family. Those few who speculate on the future of the family have also been generally inclined to limit their predictions to changes occurring in the family life of the middle classes. Their scenarios reflect the future of families like "The

Jetsons," the television cartoon characters whose suburban
life style is already geared (or rather, wired), to the
space age.

The purpose of this paper is to compare the future of
the poor and of the more affluent middle-class families, in
light of the ways they have coped with industrial capitalism
in the past. We will review the emergence of the nuclear
family, and the extent to which the middle-class model has
been the sole basis for predictions of change in the American family. Likewise we will preview the yet unwritten
history of the lower-class family and its probable future.

To a great extent, middle-class families are currently
being confronted with problems similar to those faced by
poor families in the past and present. It is the central
thesis of this paper that the ability of poor families to
cope with economic exigencies (e.g., recurrent unemployment,
the need for a mother's wage, etc.), to build cooperative
networks, and to transcend biology in building intimate
relationships (Kanter) can teach us a great deal about the
future of the American family in general, and the shaping
of public policies affecting the family.

Recently, Kenneth Keniston, Executive Director of the
Carnegie Council on Children, and a well-known expert on
family and child welfare policy, wrote an article in the New
York Times entitled, "The Emptying Family." (1) In this
article, Keniston argues that the exaltation of children
and the prolonged retention of children within the nuclear
family--values which he believes to be characteristic to
American society--are in a state of decline. Keniston fears
that the modern middle-class family is emptying out--
actually losing its members. He sees that fewer people
than ever are at home to raise children, that "more than
half of school-age children now have mothers who work outside the home, mostly full time." He concludes that women's
work is associated with divorce, and has caused parents to
rear children without spouses. Ultimately, Keniston equates
the rising employment of women outside the home, and divorce,
with the destruction of the family.

The family of reference here is, of course, the nuclear
family--the intense, introspective, privatized family of
Freud, God-given, natural unit of society which is charged
to cradle the search for happiness amidst the perils of the
industrial bureaucratic metropolis. And, Keniston's primary concern is the structural change occurring within the
American family that leaves fewer people at home to raise
children.

Concerning this fear over the future of the family we must, however, ask how changes in the size and structure of the family have altered its affective ties and emotional arrangements? Well, in the first place, our national "Child-centeredness" is a familial characteristic of fairly recent vintage. According to John Demos, only infants in Plymouth Colony were indulged and cherished (2). Children older than one year innocently bore the brutalities of parents who were determined to break individual spirit. Using young children as servants and apprentices severed the ties of childhood and the residential bond to the family of origin, and cast these young into adult molds. John and Virginia Demos claim that the notion of adolescence was not conceived until after 1880. They attribute its advent to rising urbanization. Children in cities, released from the chores of the farm, were allotted longer periods of dependency and parental control.

When Keniston speaks of the "emptying family," we must understand that he is speaking of the middle-class nuclear family, a relatively recently evolved social form. Somewhat paradoxically, Keniston blames economics for the depopulation of nuclear families. But the families which face the harsh-est economic realities--the poor--appear to be the ones with the stronger kinship ties. In reviewing an excellent series on the history of the nuclear family in the New York Review of Books last year, the historian Christopher Lasch has observed that "the study of family structures is of no importance unless it can be shown that an extended family creates a radically different set of emotional arrangements from the ones fostered by a nuclear family." (3) Likewise, what do we assume, and what do we know about the relation-ship between family size and structure on the one hand, and the changing fabric of inter-personal relationships within the family, on the other? Are the same trends apparent across the grid of class, and do numerical changes have the same meaning for the affluent as they do for the poor?

Background

Let us look briefly at the historians' interpretations of the impact of industrialism on the families of steadily employed workers of the emerging middle classes. With the transition to wage labor and the separation of the home and work place, a new form of family developed among steadily employed workers. Michael Anderson's study of Lanchashire cotton towns of the mid-19th century suggests that the industrial revolution led to a strengthening of kinship ties, and an increase in co-residence of parents and married children (4). Likewise, for the working classes

in contemporary society, sociologists have challenged the
view that the nuclear family is isolated from kin. But for
the middle classes in the 20th century, few scholars deny
a decline in the practical or pragmatic importance of kinship ties. Some historians, Laslett (5) and Demos, for
example, date the rather isolated nuclear family far back,
claiming that it has pre-industrial origins. Others have
challenged these interpretations on the basis of method-
ology, questioning whether legitimate demographic interpretations can be based upon a static point in time, or on the
life cycles from generation to generation. Whether historians date the shift from an extended to a nuclear faimly
as a precondition rather than a product of industrialization,
there is little doubt about the general long-term trend
toward a considerable reduction in the size of families.

Researchers attach different labels and values to the
reduction in the size of the family, the isolation of the
family unit, and the ideology of the "movement toward
autonomy and inclusion" (Lasch p. 37). Richard Sennett
takes his examples from wage-earning families in Chicago
who moved away from the inner city in the 1890's (6). In
Families Against the City (1970) Sennett describes the
search of small family units for privacy and independence--
the process of families turning inward. Sennett writes,

> "Thus, when we talk about the 'privatisation' of
> the family experience in the 19th century, we are
> on one hand talking about a belief that the family
> ought to be removed from the tremors of the outer
> world, and be a moral sphere higher than that
> outer world."

On a similar theme Lasch writes (7),

> "If the nuclear family served the needs of a market
> society based on competition, individualism, and
> Emersonian "self-reliance," it did so, . . . not by
> providing sons with appropriate 'role-models,' but
> by cutting itself off from the extended kinship group
> and the world of work. The family's isolation gave
> the relations between parents and children a new
> intensity, which enabled the young to become more
> fully autonomous than before, even as it increased
> the psychic costs of socialization. It was not so
> much the internal structure of the family that changed
> as its relations to the outside world. As an insti-
> tution defined above or as a refuge--a private re-
> treat--the family became the center of a new kind of
> emotional life, a new intimacy and inwardness."

Lasch continues,

"What mattered was the emotional intensification
of family life, which strengthened the child's
identification with his parents. This at once
sharpened the struggle necessary to achieve
autonomy and gave it a stronger basis by forcing
the individual to develop inner resources instead
of relying on external direction."

For families of the present generation, Sennett suggests
that privatisation in the 19th century sense has ceased to
exist. "The pressure dividing family experience in people's
minds from the experience of work and adult social life
does continue; in fact, there is some evidence that in the
last forty years the gap has grown wider between the actions
which middle-class adults believe make them good parents and
the actions which they construe as making them powerful, or
at least powerful enough to survive in the world." Sennett
suggests that the elements of personality and the focus on
the self has so changed in this century that people, for
example, are not willing to make great sacrifices for the
sake of preserving a marriage as a social contract. Liberation from repression has come to be couched in terms of a
liberation of the self--the so-called "wish to be free."
Yet "when people rebel against a bad marriage, it is not
usually to go live alone in the world, but rather for the
sake of, or in the hope of, finding a newer, more emotionally satisfying mate." (8)

In this sense, the family is perceived of as both
socially withdrawn and emotionally complete. Rather than
transforming the family itself, the dominance of the family
is reinforced. "As long as warm intimate relations are
given such moral priority, familism will continue, no matter
how frequently people divorce and remarry, no matter how
unusual their sexual practices, no matter how many affairs
they conduct in search of someone who 'understands' them."

These scholars describe the process of change in the
19th and 20th century family. By the mid-20th century, the
middle-class family had changed its relation to the outside
world, and become the center of a new kind of emotional
life, a refuge, a private retreat. But, in what way is this
process continuing today? Do current statistics on the
American family once again reflect a transformation in the
relation of the family to its outside environment, or do
they suggest a significant transformation of the family
itself?

Economic Considerations

The location of families in the economic hierarchy clearly influences their members' attitudes towards kinship, work, and the rights and responsibilities of the individual. Yet, the burgeoning of historical studies addressing the rising middle-class family have not been accompanied by historical studies of the families of the poor and powerless. In addition, until recently, those few who have projected backward to view the slave family, (9) or the adjustment of European peasants or rural whites and blacks to city life have largely ignored or been blind to the many collective bases of families of immigrant Italians, Irish, English, and of slave families in the New World. Interpretations largely project the experiences of the middle-class scholars who themselves extoll individualistic values and experience.

We cannot argue, as the sociologist William Goode has, that individualistic family values and ideologies have been an "independent" force in social change (10). Quite to the contrary, we must examine the experiences of peasants and laboring families in light of their place in the economy and "their familial values and not our individualistic ones." In one of the few already drafted chapters in the otherwise unwritten history of the changes that affected peasant and laboring women's work and women's place in the family in the late 19th-early 20th centuries is the work of Joan Scott and Louise Tilly. Scott and Tilly argue that "the families whose wives and daughters constituted the bulk of the female labor force in Western Europe during most of the 19th century did not value the rights and responsibilities of the individual," as Goode claims.

The relatively unexplored history of this era has permitted the assumption that the structure and function of the family is uniform regardless of class. Similarly, the unexplored history of the poor and powerless has sustained much confusion about the "history of women's work outside the home and the origin and meaning of women's traditional place within the home." (11) In contrast to the burgeois ideology of the family—and of women in particular as separated off from the sphere of goods production—the historical work of Scott and Tilly reveals that "the poor and powerless in pre-industrial society had values that fully justified the employment of women outside the home." Scott and Tilly convincingly demonstrate that "peasants and laboring families did not find feminity and economic functions incompatible."

In examining the history of the families of laborers
and the unemployed, and their families as they exist today,
we must focus attention on two basic issues. First, we
must come to understand the family as a critical component
in society's organization of production; as a fundamental
part of the "economy." Second, we must uncover the values
and the emotional arrangements of families in poverty.

In an article on the comparative effects of imperialism
and industrialism on the family, Caulfield argues that the
dichotomization of production particular to colonialism
"makes possible a sexual divide-and-rule policy: the
domestic sphere of activity is in general devalued in the
ruling-class ideology, thus lowering the status of women
and their work." (12) Because our own culture generally
accepts this devaluation, Caulfield suggests that we have
failed to note the response to oppression of families in
colonial and neo-colonial situations. Under the leadership
of women, and men, families have fought back, cemented
familial bonds, and built networks of mutual support which
are essential to the development of what Caulfield calls
"cultures of resistance." Family-based "cultures of
resistance" have arisen in the colonial world, but as
Caulfield points out, they also have been found in internal
colonial situations in the United States: in the survival
strategies of slaves; (13) in kinship-based clans in
Appalachia; (14) in the security acquired by Chicago
migrants whose conjugal families are buttressed by respon-
sive relatives; (15) and in the stable and resourceful kin-
based networks of urban women in black families in the
United States (16).

Between 1968 and 1971, I conducted a 3-year study of a
group of urbanized blacks, living principally on welfare
in a small midwestern city I call the Flats (17). Black
families living in the Flats are a part of a larger social
and economic environment from which they are relatively
isolated, but which influences their daily lives in ways
over which they have little control. Owing to unemployment, segregated housing and educational patterns, as well
as social patterns (e.g., stigma on interracial marriage),
blacks are not well integrated into the overall economy.
Despite the hardships, they have developed economic and
social mechanisms, which differ markedly from those of the
predominantly middle-class white society in which they are
embedded. They have learned to survive highly unpredict-
able social and economic conditions, which are not only
largely unresponsive to their daily needs, but which fluc-
tuate so greatly as to force continual rearrangements in
household composition.

Irregular employment restricts an individual's ability to predictably contribute to the household income. Further, although welfare provides a meager but steady income, the regulations of the welfare bureaucracy tend to discourage the possibility to develop an equity. In order to cope with all the disruptive influences in their environment, people in the Flats have developed extended networks of economically cooperative kin and friends. These networks extend well beyond household boundaries and represent relatively stable social relationships which are maintained in the face of uncertain economic conditions and fluctuations in daily economic status. Consequently, reciprocal exchanges tend to provide economic stability and a reasonable degree of economic security. While the individual cannot control the average amount of income available to him, he can, through reciprocal exchange, reduce the fluctuations and, therefore, cushion the short-term economic hardships which would otherwise ensue. These networks also serve as a means of regulating the distribution of goods and services within the community to ensure that no individual is significantly worse off than anyone else.

Contrary to superficial appearances, the domestic networks of the poor are an expression of considerable economic forethought on the part of the members. The strength of a particular domestic network depends upon cooperation between adult females, between male and female kin, and between females and their childrens' fathers and fathers' kin. Close cooperation between male and female siblings who share the same household or live near one another has been underestimated by those who have identified an isolated femaleheaded household as the most significant domestic unit among the urban black poor. Likewise, a man and his kin, although physically absent from the immediate household, contribute positive, valuable resources to his children, thereby enlarging the circle of people both families can count on for help.

Economic pressures among cooperating kinsmen in the black community work against the loss of either males or females--through marriage or long-term relationships--from the kin network. Female members of a network may act to break up a relationship that has become a drain on their resources. On the other hand, a man is expected to participate in his own kin network, and it is assumed that he should not dissipate his services and finances in a marital relationship. Clearly, kin regard any marriage as a risk to the woman and her children, and the loss of male or female kin as a threat to the durability/economic integrity of the overall kin network. Forms of social control against

marriage emanating from the larger society are reinforced
by sanctions within the Flats. At the same time, a woman
will continue to seek aid from the man (men) who has (have)
fathered her child(ren), thus building up her own network's
resources. She also expects something from his kin,
especially his mothers and sisters. Women continually
activate these lines to bring kin and friends into their
network of exchange and obligation. Most often, the biological father's female relatives are also poor, and also
try to expand their network and increase the number of
people they can depend on. All of these strategies tend
to maximize and maintain long-term relationships within
domestic networks.

Current Implications

Given the striking contrast between the middle-class
celebration of individualism and the reliance on familism
among the poor, let us re-examine the implications of
recent statistics on the American family.

In 1975, two out of five children had mothers in the
labor force, the number of divorces in America passed the
one-million mark for the first time in the nation's history,
and almost half of the mothers in single-parent families
are working, a third of them, full time. The national
marriage rate has been dropping by about 4 per cent at a
time when the number of Americans of marriageable age is
increasing, and the remarriage rate among people whose
first marriage ended in divorce is tapering off. The
number of children under 18 decreased by 2.4 million, or
3.4 per cent from 1970-1974; more people live in single-
parent households than ever before and in 1975, the number
of people living alone under the age of 35 doubled.

Let us first view the meaning of these numbers in
light of the experience of the middle classes.

Isabel Sawhill has shown a correlation between women's
work and divorce. She studied the relationship between
marital stability and income, and found that there is a
"negative association between female income and marital
stability." "Each one thousand dollar increase in wife's
earnings," Sawhill writes, "leads to a one percentage
point increase in the separation rate. . . ." (18)

In fairness, we should relate this finding to Keniston's
notion of the depopulation of the middle-class family.
Granted, there has been an increase in the number of single-
parent households, the number of people who choose to live

alone, and the number of couples who choose not to have
children. These patterns reveal a self-interested detach-
ment, and atomism of the middle classes in contemporary
society. These patterns may also be said to represent the
results of the historical progression from the division
of labor within the family, to the isolation of the conjugal unit and the oppression of women.

On the other hand, middle-class and working parents who
are living in single-parent households have many needs in
common. Like their poor counterparts, they too are finding
one another. Until recently, many divorced, white, working
mothers continued to live in the suburban neighborhoods of
their marriages with few opportunities to find help for
themselves or their children. But today, single mothers
are not nearly as isolated from mainstream norms as they
were a few years ago. Single, white, mothers--widows and
those divorced and separated--are beginning to form support
networks. Widows' clubs and "parents without partners"
have very common needs, and have created responses to those
needs, even if they are not facing financial difficulties.
Many single parents share childcare, their meals, and rely
on an emotionally supportive network of friends. Among the
divorced, even noncustodial parents who live nearby are,
on occasion, a part of these networks and readily participate in their children's lives.

Rosabeth Kanter sees many such forms of family
emerging. The major factor which all such forms have in
common is what Kanter calls "the transcendence of biology
in building intimate relationships." She is joined by
several others who predict that the extended kin-friendship
networks that were so supportive to families in the past
will re-emerge in the future, but will be created by choice
rather than by ties of blood and kinship.

Do these forms of family life, which are relatively
new to the middle classes, represent a radically different
set of emotional arrangements within the family? Kanter
and others appear to believe that current changes in the
family and the variations in family life styles--communes,
contractual relationships, child-free marriages, etc.--
represent a "transitional stage to a future where the family
will have a different form altogether." Before we decide
whether these variations of the family represent a radical
difference, let us look more closely at the role of women's
work, and other issues, among the poor.

As with the middle class, the number of poor single-
parent households rose during the past decade and more than

half of the mothers in single-parent families are working.
For black women, the U.S. Census has probably underestimated
the participation of black women in the labor force. Nevertheless, the Women's Bureau of the U.S. Department of Labor
has found that black women have been represented in the
American labor force longer, and in greater numbers than
their white counterparts (DeAlemeida).

Without a doubt, as Eleanor DeAlemeida has shown,

Black women's work force participation has been
a critical variable affecting the survival and
mobility of black Americans (Hill: 1972). In
1970, 47.5% of all black women over 16 years of
age were in the labor force. 38.2% of black
women who were married (spouse present) were in
the labor force. 48.1% of these women were in
families with children under 6, while 58.4% had
children between 6 and 17 years of age. In 1970
the average contribution of these women to their
families' income was 33%. How then, can we
ignore her contribution to the social placement
of her offspring?

Black women have always worked and still expect to work.
In contrast to Kiniston's worries, the work of black women
has not depopulated or emptied the black family. Furthermore, the work of black women has not left an empty or
"latch-key" household for children. Black children are
reared at home among many caring kin. Shared adult responsibilities toward children in the black community are not only
an obligation of kinship, they constitute a highly cherished
right.

Needless to say, the chronic unemployment of black men
has a profound effect on marital stability among the poor.
Judging from case histories and statistical data, there is
no doubt that among low-income blacks, an increase in male
earnings has a stabilizing impact on the family. In a study
by Isabel Sawhill of over five thousand households and their
economic fortunes, Sawhill found a positive correlation
between male income and marital stability.

With this broader social-economic perspective, can we
now say that the increase in the number of working mothers
and the rise in the divorce rate must necessarily lead to an
elimination of the family, or rather, to its transformation?
I believe that the latter is the case rather than the
former.

We have seen examples of the profound respect for
women's work or transfer income in poor families, and the
adaptive strategies built around women's wage labor within
poor families in the 19th and 20th century. Likewise we
are seeing examples of the re-emergence of intimate, cooperative networks among middle-class parents and non-
parents. Considered out of context, facts and figures on
the rise of female-headed households and working mothers
in the U.S. middle class may rightfully generate serious
concern. But, by identifying an analogue of current trends
within the socio-economic histories of other cultures and
classes, it becomes apparent that present generations are
experimenting with "tried and true" solutions to their
problems.

While it is difficult to hypothesize the long-term
implications of current trends, we can reach one significant
conclusion. Middle-class individuals and families, like
their poor counterparts, are resilient, flexible, and
creative. They, too, are capable of optimizing situations
to suit their needs. Few individuals or families are
fragile, though many are poor. In times of stress, when
employers and governments cut back on jobs and services,
all families respond by creating their own appropriate
technologies. What is clear is that when our society can
offer a self-respecting livelihood to individuals, families
take care of themselves. This is what families do well.
Our public policies need to recognize the strengths of
families who have had economic opportunities, and the
economic origins of the problems of families who appear to
be in trouble. Family strengths are rooted in economic
opportunities, and family problems stem from socially
caused poverty. Our public policies must be designed
around this fact.

References

1. Keniston, Kenneth, "The Emptying Family," New York Times, February 18; 37:2 and February 20; 33:2, 1976, (series of articles).

2. Demos, John, A Little Commonwealth: Family Life in Plymouth Colony (New York: Oxford University Press, 1970).

3. Lasch, Christopher, "The Emotions of Family Life," New York Book Review, November 27, 1975: 37-41.

4. Anderson, Michael, Family Structure in Nineteenth Century (Lancashire, Cambridge, England: Cambridge University Press, 1971).

5. Laslett, Peter, Introduction: The History of the Family In Peter Laslett and Richard Wall, Household and Family in Past Time (Cambridge, England: Cambridge University Press, 1972), pp. 1-89.

6. Sennett, Richard, Families Against the City: Middle Class Homes of Industrial Chicago (Cambridge, Massachusetts: Harvard University Press, 1970).

7. Lasch, Christopher, "The Family and History," New York Review of Books, November 13, 1975: 33-8.

8. Sennett, Richard, The Fall of Public Man, p. 32.

9. Gutman, Herbert, Black Family in Slavery and Freedom 1750-1925 (New York: Pantheon Books, 1976).

10. Yorburg, Betty, The Changing Family (New York: Columbia University Press, 1973), p. 105.

11. Scott, Joan and Louise Tilly, "Woman's Work and the Family in Nineteenth Century Europe" In Charles Rosenberg, The Family in History (University of Pennsylvania Press, Philadelphia), 1975, pp. 145-78.

12. Caulfield, M.D., Imperialism, the Family and Cultures of Resistance Socialist Revolution, 1974.

13. Gutman, Herbert G., The Black Family in Slavery & Freedom, 1750-1925 (New York: Pantheon Books, 1976).

14. Beaver, Patricia, unpublished Ph.D., Duke University, "Symbols and Social Organization in an Appalachian Mountain Community," 1976.

15. Williams, Bret, unpublished Ph.D., University of Illinois, "The Trip Takes Us: Chicano Migrants on the Prairie," 1975.

16. Stack, Carol B., All Our Kin: Strategies for Survival in the Black Community (New York: Harper and Row, 1974).

17. Ibid.

18. Sawhill, Isabel V., Income and Marital Instability, 1975 (Unpublished manuscript).

5

Familiar Groups as Molecules of Society

A rewritten version of remarks by Gregg
Edwards, prepared by David P. Snyder

Introduction

An underlying paradox of social policy is that both
"big" and "small" have just claims, but each tends to clobber
the other in staking those claims. Our point today is that
only by learning to respect the contributions of one
another -- individuals and institutions, public and private
sectors -- can our common national enterprise prosper and
mature. This requires avenues of collaboration -- information networks -- and habits of using them. Modern technology can provide the former; social policy can provide
opportunities and incentives for the latter.

Just Claims of the Small: Vitality. At the turn of the
century and the height of the industrial revolution, the
family and the small community were both commonly viewed by
the intellectual press as being imminently threatened by the
growth of huge organizations such as big business and state
bureaucracies which could mobilize massive power to awe and
intimidate individuals and their human scale institutions.
Thus, in 1897, Emile Durkheim concluded that we must set up
intermediate institutions between individuals and the mega-
institutions -- "collective forces outside the state,
reconstituted corporations . . . close enough to the facts
. . . to detect their nuance, and sufficiently autonomous
to . . . respect their diversity." (1) Durkheim hoped that
such human scale groups, with decentralized and therefore
credible authoritativeness, might permit the continued
vitality of human communities in the industrial era.

Durkheim explained the just claims of the small, and based
those claims on the valid needs that arise from the factual
diversity of reality: small groups can take the general

The opinions expressed herein do not necessarily reflect
those of the National Science Foundation.

values, ideas, and rules suggested by their culture or by the
state, and make them work. This is because small groups can
learn about the irregularities of their local situation and
can develop methods of coping for continued productivity.
Because productivity can be seen from individual actions and
can have collective and immediately noticeable impacts,
individuals become emotionally and socially committed to
investing themselves in small groups for continued implementation of the given, global patterns and local fixes.
Durkheim did not articulate the just claims of the larger,
collective forces in society in ways by which they might be
balanced off against the claims of the small; rather he
left this critical aspect of the social system to evolve
out of necessity and the wisdom of collective sentiment.

A fundamental function of social policy is to balance
the competing claims of big and small entities. To do this,
we must be able to discern the elements, processes, and
functions of the larger scale dynamics of social change. A
generation before Durkheim, Marx lamented the encroachments
of industrialism upon the fabric of society, and their consequences for the individual. But again, because Marx did not
perceive a process by which these competing interests might
be resolved, he postulated adjudication by the state,
initially made up of an elite of those affected. Thirty
years later, after seeing that the creation of somewhat
representative nation-states had not been sufficient to
redress the imbalance between large and small, Durkheim
prescribed his "intermediaries."

As they have been realized, Durkheim's "intermediaries"--
e.g., cooperatives, planned and intentional communities,
special group (e.g., the elderly) housing, etc. -- have been
only marginally and transiently successful, largely because
their managing elites have not had the understandings of how
to organize and operate in ways that meaningfully engage their
members to form real small communities that are comprehensive and credible enough to win their members' long-term
commitment to each other and to their common posterity. In
society at large, such commitments arise most often within
the timeless cultural contexts -- the church, ethnicity, and
above all, the loose-knit networks of kin and friends that
help each other throughout life. These natural analogues to
Durkheim's "human scale intermediaries" are not formally
acknowledged by our society or polity; in fact, they
currently find themselves extensively at odds with the complex demands of their necessary interactions with public and
private sector bureaucracies whose logics and utilities they
cannot comprehend, and which do not comprehend them. In sum,
80 years after Durkheim and 110 years after Marx, the problem
of balancing the interests of big and small in our society

remains unresolved and troublesome.

Just Claims of the Large: Fostering the Small. Marx and Durkheim prescribed institutions to solve the problem of social balance -- a state run by representatives of the underdogs, and a localized community based on collective productivity and the realistic common culture that would emerge. These prescriptions were based upon a model of social process, and a vision of how people should live. As such, they may be interpreted as part of our hope for a social science based upon the successes of physical science and engineering; to develop a model of the situation -- including the consequences desired -- and to choose parameter settings of the various available components in order to achieve the desired consequences. Marx and Durkheim hoped that their models and the resultant institutions would facilitate the lives of individuals and smaller groups, both singly and collectively.

The just claims of society's large institutions rest upon their ability to provide a valid and worthwhile model for collective interaction throughout society, and upon the net value of the additional socio-economic output derived from the application of that model, as compared with any other available model. But, as economic and social factors change over time, a particular model may not remain as valid (i.e., predictive) or as worthwhile (i.e., its consequences popularly valued) as it once was. Just as Durkheim perceived that the legitimacy of his intermediary communities lay in their ability to adapt to the different factualities of time, place and circumstance, so too, the legitimacy of our dominant institutions' model for collective interaction -- our social policy -- rests upon our ability to maintain or enhance the validity and valued consequences of that model over time.

This suggests that social policy should stand in a symbiotic, cybernetic relationship to society, in order to provide a continuously reoptimizing model for collective interaction. To do this, social policy must first inform itself of the full range of family/friendship networks and collaborations, so that it may better understand and facilitate productive interaction throughout society. In addition, social policy must inform society at large concerning the relative effectiveness of the array of family forms and other small group collaboratives in coping with the universe of circumstances and in achieving desirable outcomes. In this context, the ultimate value of social policy lies with its ability to foster effective social innovation and adaptation in response to changing economic, technologic and environmental realities.

It is not the purpose of this paper to debate the specific forms of institutions and categories of behavior for specific issues -- like abortion, welfare eligibility, preservation of aspects of ethnicity . . . but rather to examine the context of the basic function of families (which we take to be the nurturance of human development) and thereby suggest a framework for the formulation of social policy. The nature of current debates and conflicts in the area of family policy show its special complexity: the inter- action of biological processes, public policy, individual and group investments, collective education, and scientific method. In this chapter, we will try to elucidate how these factors may be tied together and how our current knowledge may better inform family policy.

The Recombinant Household: Family Adaptation to Change

The current concern over the long-term diminution of the American family provides an excellent point of departure for an examination of the social-cultural dynamic. A review of the demographics of the developed Western nations clearly shows that the decline in the size and duration of the nuclear family is a general trend, and that some nations precurse the United States in diminishing family size and fertility rates (e.g., Germany, Sweden, United Kingdom). Further, studies of social indicators suggest that there is a high correlation between dropping average family size and the rise in a number of other factors -- urbanization, in- dustrialization, average per capita income, etc. Since, by and large, these societies have not been subjected to any compulsory or coercive family reduction policies, we must assume that this course of action -- family diminution -- is being adopted voluntarily by individuals in pursuit of some mix of perceived utilities or satisfactions.

In fact, the literature generally supports the view that within the basic, Western European/North American family pattern (monogamous, patriarchial), there has been wide variation according to circumstances. In troubled times, Elise Boulding notes that a very substantial fraction of women in Europe lived and raised children in large, communal "beguines" from the 12th to the 16th centuries (2). Aries reports strong shifts in family-styles as befitting the times: when the larger social structure is uncertain, people bond together in tight, extended families; in more secure times, the restrictions and discomfortures of close living tend to push the nuclear, reproductive units apart (3). Laslett suggests that the details of child rearing shifted with changing familial circumstances as a precurser and facilitator of industrialization (4). In surveying 200 years

of changes in the family roles of American children, Kett
found that juveniles shifted from being economic participants
to work-force preparants (5). And, in extending the examination of family metamorphosis to non-Western societies,
Laslett records similar survival strategies adopted by cultures with radically different ideals for family structure;
for example, the simple, small, loving families of Japan's
Hilda, and the extended families of India's urban Hindi (6).
Both took a mixed solution -- nuclear plus adopted kin
groups -- apparently to gain a shared higher value: the
conservation of family name and status despite difficult
circumstances.

Social Evolution, Social Policy and the Social Contract

Thus, it appears that the primary social group --
"family" -- is an adaptive form which adjusts to the
realities of its environment. But what role does public
policy play vis-a-vis this process? What are the rights and
necessities which entitle our collective institutions to set
social standards or policies that impact upon the structure
and dynamics of our social system? These entitlements of
government rest upon the two basic commonalities that constitute a society -- common agreements and common resources.

Our common agreements are the consensual values,
expectations and perceptions of reality from which society
creates the network of institutions and mechanisms to employ
its resources to the maximum mutual benefit of its members.
These common agreements are subject to generational change.
Succeeding generations contribute to and consume society's
common resources in different manners and at proportionally
different rates. This requires constant adjustments in the
distribution of scarce resources. Taken together, these
common resources and agreements form the altruistic base of
society upon which the validity of the state rests. Government is the collective tool of the common endeavor to achieve
the best allocation of its resources, and the legitimacy of
government is directly related to its effectiveness in this
task.

These roles and relationships seem familiar enough; they
represent the fundamental elements of the social contract.
But the idea of the social contract, by itself, inadequately
defines the imperatives of governance because it does not
explicitly take time into account; it does not acknowledge
society in a dynamic, evolutionary context. Yet, as the
common resource base and the consensual agreements of a
society change over time, imponderable but unignorable issues
arise regarding the allocation of resources. If the society

is to survive and prosper, patterns of social investment cannot remain frozen by the dead hand of yesterday's intents or
perceptions. Studies of ecosystems and economic institutions
alike provide us with ample evidence of the imperatives of
change.

Out of the imperatives of social and economic change
arises an important specialization of concern which characterizes government's contribution to the common enterprise.
While individuals and institutions may be primarily concerned
with the survival and prosperity of themselves and their own
interests, government must be primarily concerned with the
survival and prosperity of the whole. The current generation, in the sum of its collaborative and competitive
pursuits, does not have the right to dissipate the common
inheritance from its forbears, nor to prohibitively encumber
the birthright of its children. Thus, government's responsibility for the continuity of the collective enterprise
transcends the interests of individuals and institutions,
generations and ethnicities.

Within this overall framework, the potential for conflict is implicit. Familiar groups, along with other institutions, seek to adapt to their changing circumstances in
order to prosper and survive. As the cost of living soars,
more adult members of the household seek employment, and
individual adults seek additional work. As the emotional and
economic burden of child-rearing increases, some families
commit themselves to fewer offspring, and seek government
measures to reduce their burden. On an even more fundamental
level, individuals who perceive that traditional family forms
offer diminished utilities -- e.g., rewards or security --
experiment with new primary group forms which they believe
offer better prospects for their survival and satisfaction.
Among these are the individuals who perceive the family to be
so inutile or problematical an institution that they eschew
it altogether, choosing instead for primary community the
less formal networks of social, professional and avocational
peers, and the support of large scale service institutions --
singles apartment complexes, health and unemployment insurance, welfare, etc.

From the free exercise of individual choice, the social
structure adjusts to circumstances in order to serve the
utilities of its members, from these changes, disagreements
and conflicts arise. How shall we allocate our common resources? Shall we give premium welfare payments to families
who remain united? Shall we increase our investments in
social security in anticipation of growing dependence upon
that system? Shall we support institutional parenting

through tax deductions for the child care of working parents? Shall we pay for -- or even permit -- abortions; if not, who shall bear the cost for the unwanted children? Social policy, reflecting the common agreements of prior generations, is challenged by adaptive behaviors of members of the contemporary generation. To maintain its legitimacy, government must provide for the just resolution of these conflicts and for the orderly management of the resulting change.

Current social policy seems ill-suited either to resolve conflict or to facilitate orderly social change. Having focused its attention on a limited array of familial forms (e.g., single persons, childless married couples, married and single parents), it lacks knowledge of the contemporary social dynamic. While ample data is collected, for example, on marriages, births, and divorces, little information is gathered concerning the formation, growth, performance and attrition of other household or institutional group forms. For example, we barely acknowledge the extended family network of the urban poor described by Dr. Stack elsewhere in this volume, and we collect no data at all that would reflect how well these or other non-normative familiar groups provide for one another, or the extent to which such forms of collaboration contribute to our society. As Dr. Allen observes in Chapter 1, such forms do not fit our demographic standards.

Social policy both fosters and suffers from its ignorance of the social dynamic. Further, society itself is left ignorant of the performance of evolving, experimental familial forms. Thus, in choosing to assay some alternative form of primary group, members of society have no sense of the relative success, stability or failure of such forms. Nor do they know how or what these forms of social enterprise contribute or detract from the greater society, or how well they satisfy the needs and expectations of their members. If we do not know how the various elements of society are contributing to or taking from the common resources, then government is ill-equipped to determine the best allocation of those resources. Similarly, if we do not understand how, and how well, our various primary groups and institutions support their members and the greater society, government is ill-equipped to resolve the conflicts arising out of the social policy debate or to assure orderly social change and continuity.

It is apparent, then, that both society and its government need a much better understanding of the social dynamic and what is happening within that dynamic in order to make intelligent inter-generational investments of its financial and human resources. Fortunately, with the emergence of the

appropriate partners as nuclear breeding pairs. Earlier, it
was asserted that historical and cross-cultural surveys
reveal a tendency for such breeding nucleii to evolve toward
matured familiar forms that are most appropriate to their
circumstances. But by what process are such alternative
family-styles and their relative merits made known to the
individual members of society? Does the research base
suggest a source for evolving perceptions of appropriate
family forms and functions? It appears to!

In their world-wide cross cultural analysis, Minturn and
Lambert, found great variation in family and brooding styles
(9). Further, it has been demonstrated that the key factors
of stylistic difference vary complexly with other cultural
elements (Sawyer and Levine (10); Barry (11)). Within this
rich variation, the dominent interest of the family group is
in preparing children to take roles in the expected world
while maintaining respect for traditional core values. The
Whitings found that family structures of all kinds inculcate
particular personal roles and styles in their offspring, a
process which begins at infancy and is largely completed by
the age of six years (12). Such styles are taught to help
the child later in society, and in particular, to set up
their own households which will continue that style (Barry
(13)). Thus, mothers in simple societies work at home,
encourage responsibilities for survival tasks and cooperation
with friends, while mothers at home in complex societies
encourage the dependency and competitiveness necessary for
later achievement in such an environment. Miller presents
filmed interviews with representative kin in 6 different
cultures, all of whom express concern over preparing their
children for the future while respecting the central values
of the past (14).

Thus, families themselves appear to have a significant
(perhaps pre-eminent) role in shaping each new generation's
perception of the most appropriate family style; what is
more, the data suggest that the core values and functional
human behaviors which families induce in their children have
major self-fulfilling consequences not only on their later
life-style choices, but also on their personal behavioral
styles and general mental abilities. Kagan studied the
behavior and abilities of children in an American city, and
found major differences in mental abilities directly proportional to the social class of their households; these
differences begin at age 2 and diverge at differing rates
thereafter (15). Kagan suggests, by pointing to a cross-
cultural study, that these different rates in mental advancement were due to degrees of authoritarian family structure
rather than wealth. Bernstein found similar results in

London -- pervasive differences in mental ability, modes of
speech, planning and attitudes towards people -- all elements
of personal behavioral style which he links, again, to family
structure and child-rearing (16).

From these findings, we can begin to perceive the
fundamental manner by which the family contributes to the
ongoing structure of society. People tend to choose friends
and environs which match their attitudes and abilities,
thereby to minimize pressures for personal change. In a long
series of studies, Astin has found that people choose -- and
are chosen by -- colleges, careers, and ultimately job
"success" rankings -- that are similar to, and comfortable
with their childhood background and values (17). Stern found
that people choose specific jobs and companies for the same
reason (18). Kantor, and Cohen and March found that high
management jobs are given on the same basis (19, 20). In
effect, through the enculturation of their offspring,
families shape human "pegs" who are well suited to fit some
social and economic "holes" or roles, and less suited to
others.

If attitude systems and behavioral styles induced by
households upon their children reflect expectations for the
future, as Emile Brunswick and Triandis suggest they do (21,
22), then the relative performance -- success -- of each
generation's mix of mental and personal styles provides the
basis for confirmation and continuation, or denial and dis-
couragement of those attitudes and behaviors. The contribution of this dynamic to social stability is suggested by
Inkeles and Smith, who indicate that, absent significant
shifts in the utilities of traditional styles of behavioral
and mental functioning, groups live for generations in large
cities in modern nations without much altering their values
and concommittant thinking abilities (23).

But, while small, stable communities may survive
effectively over generations by perpetuating a narrow range
of behavioral and mental ability styles, the evidence
suggests that the functions of a larger, polymorphic society
require a richer array of personal styles. For example,
Witkin suggests that a "high" or "modern" mental ability
style is inappropriate in cases where experienced people have
dealt with a given situation for a long time, particularly
when the elements of the specific situation are not clear or
precise (24). In totally different circumstances, Zuckerman
has noted that there is a highly productive, non-theoretical
mode of mental functioning which is particularly appropriate
to fields like zoology or astronomy, where the advance of
scientific knowledge is dependent upon large accumulations of

specific detailed information and the careful exploitation
of a limited number of tools (25).

In a survey that examined thought styles and child
education throughout the world, Scribner and Coe observed
three basic styles of education, each corresponding to
different cultural types, and corresponding to differing
styles of mental functioning (26). Moreover, they found each
style to be more effective for solving certain kinds of
problems than for others. For example, children educated to
modern or high mental ability styles falsely presumed a
similarity of structure in a series of puzzles; further, such
children discovered the unique characteristics of the puzzles
much more slowly than children not educated to that high
style.

The array of different attitude and thought styles
appear to be realistic adaptations to actual circumstances,
just as the forms of familiar groups appear to reflect
realistic adaptations to environment. Some sense of why this
should be is offered by Emory and Trist's extension of
Simon's mathematical automata models (27, 28); there are
different optimum problem styles for different contexts. In
a random environment, for example, learning doesn't contribute much to the group, but collective food storage vastly
increases the probability of survival. Because complex,
polymorphic societies offer a broad range of problem-solving
contexts, it is probably more adaptive for the citizens of
such societies to possess a repertoire of styles, or at
least to understand that different situations may call for
different personal or mental functioning abilities. The
literature on leadership (Hare) seems to conclude that
different styles and values are more effectively fitted to
differing situations (29). Bernstein notes that "upper
class" kids are generally trained to use more than one
style (30).

The nature of the foregoing process, by which families
prepare succeeding generations for participation in society,
may provide some insight as to the apparent diminished
effectiveness of families in this regard, within complex
dynamic social environments. Families seek to promote the
future welfare of their offspring -- thereby to perpetuate
core values -- by inculcating such values in their children,
along with those styles of behavioral and mental functioning
that are expected to serve them best in future years. In
small, simple or stable cultures, there tend to be a relatively limited number of distinctly different social and
economic roles, the most suitable behavioral and mental
styles for which are commonly understood and constantly

new information technologies, we have the prospective capacity to acquire just such an understanding. In fact, these
technologies have already made possible an explosive increase
in social and cultural research over the past two decades,
and have thereby contributed substantially to the growing
realism of our discussions of social policy.

This paper is basically a manifestation of that urge
toward realism. The purpose here is to reconsider some very
old questions in light of these emerging realities, and to
posit that the proper purpose of social policy should not be
the support of a limited number of normative household forms,
but rather the enablement of the overall social dynamic and
the evolutionary adaptation of familiar group forms that are
most appropriate to contemporary social and economic circumstances. Finally, it will be argued that the proper context
for developing social policy can be provided by an examination of those logics which research has identified as
components of the social dynamic -- the logics which appear
to govern the formation, continuity and functioning of
families and familiar networks. From such an examination, we
may devise some experience-based extensions of common law --
a common science of social functionality to guide policy
formation.

Personal Styles and Life Roles: Family/Friendship Networks as Autonomic Agents of Social Change

Placed in the context of other biological beings, Wilson
has found humans to be among the most variable in mating,
child-rearing, and group formation habits; so variable, in
fact, that in a review of our basic social mechanisms, he
discovered human correlates for almost all those patterns
which have been used to describe basic animal group behavior
(7). This striking replication of strategies may be seen in
the similar organizations of behavior that are adopted by
enormously different animals to solve similar time and energy
allocation problems. For example, the timing, location of
arrival and duration of stay in common human "mating grounds"
(like dating bars), have been observed to follow the same
patterns as dragonflies (Platheuis Lydia), birds (grouse) and
other mammals (elephant seals), depending on the "staying
power" and "competitiveness" ranking of males and females
(8). This differentiation of behavior patterns allows time
and place slots to get sorted out so that the "best" partners
find one another, and have access to as many of the "next
best" partners as possible.

This suggests that, in the social "market place,"
natural mechanisms serve to promote the selection of mutually

demonstrated by first-hand experience. But in large, complexly diverse or dynamic cultures, the number of distinctly
different social and economic roles is quite large, and the
concommittant number and variety of utilitarian behavioral
and mental styles grows and shifts accordingly.

In such a milieu, it is much more difficult for families
or kinship networks to be knowledgeable -- through the first-
hand experience of their members -- of those styles which
possess high expected utility. Absent such knowledge,
stylistic patterning and cognitive learning must either rely
on traditional and perhaps outmoded expectations, or adapt a
certain ambivalence, which will tend to give non-family
input -- TV, schools, etc. -- greater 'weight. Thus, it would
again seem apparent that, in order to function and adapt
effectively, the social dynamic is in need of more and better
information regarding not only the relative performance of
alternative primary group forms, but also regarding the
effectiveness of different styles of behavioral and mental
functioning. Fortunately, over the past decade, research has
begun to suggest at least some of the major dimensions of
expressive and attitude styles, and by integrating them, we
may be able to better understand the functions, disfunctions,
and mutual benefits of human diversity in social evolution.

Dimensions of Personality and Mental Ability

Lomax (31) has drawn out four major dimensions of
variation in expressive style from an analysis of several
hundred cultures around the world; these dimensions, in turn,
discern about 50 major elements in a complex taxonomy which
key primarily to subsistence technologies. Lomax's major
"phyla" appear to rest on the same distinctions as those
found by Scribner and Coe (32). These major dimensions --
which, on inspection, seem quite similar to the factors of
bureaucratic style drawn out by Kantor (33) -- are not
orthogonal; further, they vary non-linearly with social complexity and technology (Lomax (34)). Thus, for example,
group solidarity has generally taken on a diminishing importance as a utilitarian element of behavioral style in more
highly technologized cultures (Lomax), but it appears to be a
key survival factor for those stopped in middle management
jobs (Kantor 35)). These dimensions of personal style also
seem very similar to those developed by Triandis in his
cross-cultural analysis of subjective culture and its
relationship to family style and social behavior (36).
Triandis' dimensions represent attitudes toward learning
about different aspects of the real world.

If we put these various models together in simple form,

they suggest a large number of variations in cultural expressive style, each of which encourages a particular mix of dimensions of mental functioning. Within each culture, there is considerable variability in the range of actual personalities -- some favored, some not. As we have seen above, there is some "resonance" between cultural dimensions and personality dimensions. In addition, Cattell notes that he has found correlations between his four fundamental factors of personality and dominant cultural belief structures (37). These also correspond well with Sorokin's four dimensions of culture, and to Morris' factored dimensions of "Ways of Life" as he has classified cultural value systems around the world (38, 39).

In sum, if we take Lomax, or Scribner and Coe's three major levels of complexity of Mental Functioning (up to industrialization), and add another layer corresponding to Piaget's fourth level -- i.e., post-industrial -- roles/tasks, and make the same addition to the other dimensions -- Personality, Belief, and Culture -- we would have a simplified 4x4x4x4 model of human diversity. Arensburg has suggested a similar scheme, in which new layers of "control" are added in conjunction with cultural growth, the coordination of which requires new sets of roles -- usually placed on top of preceding basic functions; each new set of roles, in turn, require a new set of styles (40). Toynbee suggested that, in religious communities, the natural dynamics of human personality differences tend to "fill in the boxes" of a somewhat similar model (41). Erich Neumann and Northrop Frye have separately created catalogues of characters occurring in the world's fictional literature, and fit them, on the basis of their interactions with other characters, into what appear to be similar 4x4 schemes; Frye's model is somewhat more complex, but only because he includes in his typology the prejudicial views of characters as "seen" by other characters. In both models, the characters are arrayed by hierarchies linked to different levels of social development (42, 43).

The literature is repleat with similar perceptions -- similar depictions of the patterns of human diversity -- at both the micro and macro level. Mitoff and Kilmann interviewed NASA scientists and independently found that the scientists' characterizations of themselves and each other fit the same 4x4 scheme (44). Talcott Parsons has built a theory of personality and social group development with what appears to be 16 similar characters (45). Wish and Wish report a 4-dimensional description of the interpersonal perception of differing personalities and their roles in family and friendship groups (46). Triandis, finding similar dimensions in his cross-cultural survey on role perceptions,

connects them to the attitudinal dimensions discussed earlier,
and suggests that they correspond to "trans-special" social
behavior (47).

All of the foregoing formulations are essentially equal
to one another; some identify 16 basic characters, others
identify 4, and then add the rest through character variation.
Together, they can fairly be taken to represent an approximate
internal projective logic of human beings in social situations.
Of course, the factors of this simplified scheme are based,
at least in some cases, upon groupings of hundreds of observable, lower level factors, and indeed gloss over fairly
large statistical fluctuations (see Lomax or Cattell, op.
cit.). Further, such underlying observables are often related
to the overlaying logics by complete "trees," or high-dimen-
sional connection matrices. In contemplating this implicit
theoretical structure, if we were to assign a hundred "anchors"
of reality for each parameter or scale, the combined matrix
for cultural style alone would be 100^4 -- of billion boxes or
variations.

This is clearly too vast and complex for anyone to grasp
or meaningfully use. Further, if we truly want to be
realistic in attempting to model the dynamics of human
diversity, there are similar mechanisms of interaction for
the behavioral, value/belief and mental functioning styles
in addition to cultural style. And we would have to include
all of the topological linkages among the 4 sets of
dimensions. With such a construct, we begin to approach the
outer limits of what could be stored in a computer made from
all of the matter in the visible universe (Bremmerman (48)).
In any event, we would never have time to ascertain all of
the linkages.

So great is the scale and richness of human diversity,
and so complex the mix and dynamic of personality and circumstance, that we never need worry that we may some day achieve
the capability/capacity to manage human behavior toward some
optimality; in fact, it is obviously useless to aspire to
such an end. However, to attempt to frame a rational social
policy of any sort without acknowledging this process and
attempting to understand how it affects society is needlessly
blind and foolhardy, rather like ignoring the universe simply
because we can't do anything about it.

The size of the simple 4^4 model suggested earlier -- a
256 space matrix -- is the size of Jacobsons' cross-cultural
phoneme space (49), and fits Miller's criterion of data that
can be held in short-term human memory, and thus, thought
about (50). Though aggregate and approximate, such a schema

can serve as society's first step to self-understanding.
More "realistic" models could be fabricated by concatenating
similar size "morps," or Chinese puzzles, Talcott Parsons
style. Structures of this size could serve as the elements
of a finite algebra or geometry, with all relationships
defined internally (Conway (51); Room (52)). Thus, it should
be possible to analyze and present our observations from life
in a form comprehensible to human beings as well as cal-
culable by computers. In this manner, we may regain in our
complex, diverse society some sense of how we interact --
often circuitously and at great distances of time and location -- to each others benefit; a map of our mutualities.

A comprehension of the common social enterprise and
our individual place in it are essential elements for social
functioning. Mead observed that, for a community to
function, people need to know their place in it, so that
they can function together (53). Parsons concludes his
sociological analysis of the development of modern societies
by stating that the "storm center" now is the reestablish-
ment of our "mutuality;" that is, a rational and motivational
basis for individual participation in the larger social
endeavor which would provide a perception of how one's
efforts -- inputs into a complex mega-system -- can be
expected to bring back rewards and/or push forward common
social goals (54). An equally essential aspect of such a
map of mutualism would be the depiction of how various
privileges and rewards may be legitimately earned.

Lomax has said that the intent of his world survey of
expression is to help people see how they fit into the whole,
thereby to support them with a solid base of self-dignity in
assessing their lives and making their role choices (55).
Durkheim noted that any such world view must be translatable
into the face-to-face interactions of daily living; that is,
into the family-primary group and the extended household,
and into dealing with the world outside of this context.
Without this view, people lose direction and interest in
action, because action has limited predictable utility.
Weber tracked the fall of regimes and the decline of bureaucracies to this very failure.

There is a very important message here for society and
for social policy. It says that if our conception of "family"
does not clearly convey the institution's practical, day-to-
day utility and unique personal relevancy, and further does
not explicate its role in contributing to the larger society,
it will neither sustain the family nor the society's commitment to it. This means that, to be effective, our perception
of the family must simultaneously comprehend its intimates,

its larger social and economic environment, and the interaction between the two; it must be realistic enough to be
credible in the face of contemporary daily experience and
yet broadly enough framed to provide a basis for adaptation
to change. Therefore, it is not enough to provide ourselves
with a useful sense of human diversity and interdependence;
we must also try to understand how the process of social
adaptation interacts with the universe of personality and
life-styles, shifting their relative utilities and cultural
resonance.

Here, too, the literature does provide us with some
idea of what's going on. And basically, it appears that the
dominant mode of human social evolution has been, in one form
or another, cultural "imperialism." As the top layers of a
society become more dominant, they seek to "quiet" the
expression of style of people in positions below them (Duncan
and Fiske; Birdwhistle), but not, at first, the styles of
childrearing (56, 57). Lower class children are not trained
to match the psychology of the upper classes, and thus cannot
compete for the higher positions. Brittan, for example,
finds that the high heritability of class, from generation to
generation, depends greatly upon inherited style (58).
Blocked from direct access to the dominant, more secure
layers of society, families adopt -- and inculcate in their
young -- a form of cultural "mimicry," as circumstances and
resources permit an extrapolation of the basic style patterns
of the dominant classes (Jacobs (59); Toynbee (60)). For
example, Astin reports that the Junior College system in this
country gives people the illusion of a college degree while
resulting in very little substantive difference in behavioral
or mental ability styles (61).

Now, against this process of evolving dominant "high"
styles, the continuity of more basic styles is assured by
local childrearing in some groups. This continuity provides
a sort of insurance for society against cultural collapse
brought on by faddish life-styles, ecological disasters or
the influx of barbarian conquerers. But these basic styles
function and have utility only in conjunction with self-
sufficient productivity; thus, such groups ordinarily do not
need or desire to participate in the larger society's system
of collective compromises and mutual insurance. In the past,
the preservers of the basic life-styles have maintained
continuity by living self-sufficiently on the frontiers,
along with dissident groups expelled from the industrial
cities. Today, there is almost no frontier, and tradi-
tionalist societies or dissident groups must move into the
deserts and jungles, or fight back to preserve their rights
to exist. With the global spread of industrial development

and modernization of life-styles, world society is losing
its insurance policy, and the ancient knowledges and arts
have often proven difficult to later redevelop or recreate.
This suggests that society might do well to follow Kenneth
Arrow's mathematically-derived "rational replacement rule:"
don't replace any productive machine, let it wear out first!
(62) In other words, don't force the elimination of the
functional life-styles; let them die out only from natural
loss of utility. This might entail setting up traditional
living "preserves."

Modern societies have demonstrated a strong disincli-
nation, however, to encourage or even permit great freedom
in the expression or perpetuation of style. Some modes of
child-rearing so dull or handicap offspring that they cannot
make realistic life choices, while others produce young
people who are so aggressive that they cannot work with
others. As a result, most industrial societies have chosen
to forcefully school and enculturate children to a point
sufficient for potential participation in the larger community. With continued economic development and political
maturation, both globally and domestically, the universal
achievement of a basic participative competency will
increasingly be seen as an essential goal. Some jurisdictions are exploring "competency certification" as a means
of insuring educational enculturation, while recent reports
(Kagan) of hard-to-correct, early (i.e., family) influences
on later development are currently provoking proposals for
"corrective" pre-schooling (63).

Such institutional responses to perceived social disfunctions give rise to critical issues: who shall provide
such schooling and what styles and abilities shall be
fostered? Shall employers be required to provide daycare,
or shall we encourage co-operatives? If "high" styles and
abilities are inculcated, may these not come into conflict
with the styles fostered as utilitarian by the household
environment? Perhaps, following Bernstein's observations of
middle class child rearing, both high and low styles should
be taught (64).

Current social policy, however, does not provide a
valid basis for adjudicating these issues; in cognizance of
this, the social policy process diligently eschews such
questions, or relies upon the courts to resolve them when
they cannot be avoided. Yet, society has a valid concern if
a significant portion of the population possesses mixes of
behavioral, mental or other styles which are non-inte-
gratable with, or disfunctional to, the dominant cultural
forms and systems. Barron and Kelso found that perhaps

10-15% of American adults are functionally non-competent, in
terms of mental ability styles, to effectively manage their
own lives in the contemporary socio-economic milieu; they
found another one-third of the population to be marginally
competent (65). Figures such as these, plus reports of
deteriorating overall performance on scholastic benchmark
tests, and the demands of an immature service economy for
large-volumes of literate, semi-skilled labor all combine to
enforce a potential tendency toward a stylistically polarized
society.

Most developing nations provide ample evidence of the
destabilizing influence of long-term rule by "high" style
intellectual elites over lower classes who are barred from
participation in upper and mid-level roles by their inappropriate styles and abilities, and who are barred by economic,
social or political restrictions from acquiring such tools.
Not only do such societies naturally engender internal conflict by stifling adaptive behavior toward improved circumstances on the part of the bulk of the population, but the
small, homogenous elites tend to become rigid and are unable
to cope with situations best requiring different styles.
Under such conditions, the entire culture can become fragile
and susceptible to collapse, as Flannery suggests happened
to the Meso-American civilizations (66).

To ecologists, the fundamental realities reflected in
these social concepts are familiar: under conditions of
uncertainty and environmental fluctuation, generalists with
many strategies do better than highly specialized species
(Wiens (67)). The extension of this principle of lesser life
form development to human society suggests that our "pheno-
typical expressions of plastic traits" may be our children,
our social networks -- our friends and family -- since the
evidence suggests that these are developed, through adaptation and off-spring enculturation, based upon our best
judgements; judgements which carry, in varying degrees,
information regarding impending changes in the environment.
Thus, society might do well to encourage multiple strategies
of mental functioning throughout the population, particularly
in times of significant change and uncertainty.

The Metamorphosis of Modern Societies

There is little doubt that the developed nations of the
world are currently going through times of change and uncertainty, and that our culture is being confronted with an
array of fundamental metamorphoses. The maturation of our
population represents one such set of changes. Average life
spans have increased more than a decade during the past 25

years; there are fewer children as a portion of the total
population, and their schooling, on the average, lasts more
than 50% longer than it did a generation ago. Child rearing
is completed for most women, and job ranking occurs for most
men, a decade earlier than it did a generation ago. This
means that effective, post-parenting and post-career development (i.e., 40+) adult life spans have more than doubled
since World War II, with few provisions or guidelines for
keeping the body and intellect vital beyond completion of the
initial life-choice niche; an entire second adult life with
no consensual images of obligation or purposeful occupation.

At the same time that modern societies are undergoing
these basic shifts in make-up, they are also altering some
of their fundamental needs and utilities. The most valued
human activities are less and less linked to the body -- sex,
size, agility, genetic stock, etc. -- and more and more
linked to the mind -- knowledge, intelligence, empathy and
creativity, etc. This shift from menial to mental activity
is manifested at all levels of society: in our employment,
in our daily living, and in our participation in community
and collective activities, including politics and governance.
Finally, even as society is undergoing significant alterations in its makeup and activities, it is being confronted
with multiple change and uncertainty in its physical environment; energy, pollution, social and economic infrastructure --
all are posing problematical issues for society.

Given the foregoing array of changes and uncertainties,
our understanding of the social dynamic would, indeed,
suggest that our social policy encourage not only multiple
styles of mental functioning, but also multiple behavioral
and cultural styles, in order to support appropriate social
adaptation to change. But social policy today does not
encourage such diversity. To the contrary, in our efforts to
manage modern complexity, we have evolved large bureaucracies
and mass media whose administrative convenience and sense of
equity homogenizes and equivocates (Burger (68)). Our
institutionally based social policy naturally seeks to
simplify and standardize social forms and behaviors into a
limited, clearly-defined set which can be efficiently dealt
with by mega-institutional social technologies. In so doing,
social policy serves as a bell jar placed over the bell curve
of diversity in the human ecosystem, reducing society's
natural adaptivity and producing economic stagflation and
cultural sterility.

Social Policy and Economic Stagflation

Contemporary debate over the relative rights and

obligations of society and government has generally lost
sight of the fact that it has been only recently that the two
have been regarded as distinct or separate from one another.
Before the rise of the modern nation state, large-scale
industrial technologies, and their sophisticated infrastructure requirements, society was largely a self-managed
affair in which family, clan and local community played the
dominant role in the provision of justice and governance,
and in the distribution of common resources. Over time,
society has more or less voluntarily assigned a portion of
these tasks to its public institutions, as back-ups and
supplements to family and friends.

Today, these supplemental social support mechanisms
appear to loom very large in our lives, yet they still
serve only as augmentation to the fundamental nurturance
provided by the household. Assuming minimum wage scales,
the annual value of goods and services provided within
households for their members is well over one trillion
dollars. If these same services were done at the "quality"
rates characteristic of modern service institutions -- e.g.,
nursing homes, boarding schools, etc. -- their costs would
be several times the present institutional GNP. As it is,
given the extremely high costs of our public welfare and
social service programs (roughly one half trillion dollars
for all U.S. jurisdictions), society must depend upon these
programs not being extensively used. In Great Britain, with
one of the most comprehensive social welfare systems, only
a small fraction of the potential eligible caseload of
problems are taken outside of the family-friendship nexus
(Maroney (69)).

Given an approximate 10:1 ratio in the size of the informal (family-friendship) support system versus the public
support systems, it is clear that a small shift of responsibility from the former to the latter could swamp the second,
and ultimately the entire economy. For this reason, regulating the boundry of authority between these two systems is
one of the hotter ongoing political debates in most democratic societies. What is necessary to aid this debate is
a better, more comprehensive accounting system, which focuses
not merely upon the cost, performance, and jurisdiction of
the formal social service systems, but the informal systems
as well.

For example, if we define a "dependent" as an individual
whose consumption exceeds his/her productivity or earned
income, nearly 60% of the total U.S. population is "dependent" at any one time; the bulk of these are dependent upon
the household. (This estimate, based upon U.S. government

data, probably understates the numbers of disabled and
dependent -- e.g., physically or mentally impaired,
unemployed, alcoholics, the elderly, etc. -- who reside
within households). Basically, we are a dependent society,
with the young and the elderly constituting about 3/4 of
the dependents. In 1950, the ratio of those 21 or younger
to those over 65 in our society was 4.5:1; today, it is a
little over 3:1. By 2000, the Census Bureau estimates that
the ratio of "minors" to "elders" will have dropped to
2.2-2.6:1. And, while the number of young may remain stable
or decline between now and the end of the century, the number
of people over 65 will increase by an estimated 10-12 million
(70).

Thus, while the youth dependency rate in the overall
society will be going down over the coming decades, if
current long-term trends continue, there will be an increasing tendency toward institutional stewardship of the
elderly. This shift may mean very large increases in
society's institutional costs for two reasons: prices and
expectations. We have created a system of prescribed "treat-
ments" (e.g., medical care, education, housing, pensions,
etc.) for institutional dependents, in which some tasks
may cost 10,000 times more than when they are provided by
the informal networks of family and friends. Further, mass
education and mass media have made most people highly aware
of the existence and nature of first class institutional
services, and political parties promise such services to
all who need them.

Thus, we have in motion a socio-political process under
which increasing numbers of people feel they are entitled to
a superlative standard of institutional services. The
initiation of this process was relatively easy, and made
almost everybody happy. Institutional professionals have
built increasingly structured, hierarchical delivery systems
with constantly rising costs, linked largely to high-salaried
personnel, costly technologies and procedures, and increasing
standards of performance. As a result, millions of professional and semi-professional workers have been trained
and employed, and millions of dependents have been given more
and better care.

The steadily increasing costs of "dependency displace-
ment" is already contributing to current economic stagflation.
Olken notes that institutions handle these increasing costs
by racheting up their wages and prices to maintain the status
quo in market and job situations (71). By increasing prices
at a fixed rate above labor costs, they decrease their
internal investment flows; and, by increasing wages at costs

plus "length-of-service" raises -- roughly the rate of increasing productivity -- the spiral is maintained. The
resultant inflation discourages saving and market investments
which, in turn, cuts productivity and job formation. Only
institutional dependents and those in highly organized labor
markets benefit. This discourages economic innovation,
entrepreneurship and growth.

The potential economic drag posed by the increased use
of formal social support institutions would appear to be
significant. What is more, economic stagflation from whatever cause is reinforced by feedback through the social
system. Attitude surveys indicate that having "important"
or "meaningful" work is now the most desirable job characteristic for most American white collar and younger workers
(National Opinion Research Center) (72). The significance
of work performed is currently perceived by all to be a more
attractive feature of employment than job security, working
conditions or high salary. Yet, modern institutions, with
their multiple-identical rudimentary tasks -- often many
times removed from ultimate end-products or outcomes -- are
ill-suited to provide employment which may be broadly perceived as meaningful or important. This is particularly
true in a society where the mass media provide a relatively
well-educated populace with a fairly comprehensive view of
the real world, its needs and imperatives. Thus, there is an
apparent fundamental mismatch between worker desires and much
institutional employment, as a result of which, a large segment of the population is engaged in work which does not
provide them with a personal sense of meaningful commitment
to the greater community. Absent growth or innovation in
the economic system, people are more likely to become locked
into disliked jobs or careers. Ultimately, this can be
expected to induce more people to become "dependents,"
through early retirement, voluntary unemployment, alcoholism,
etc.

It has been suggested by some that contemporary economic
policy cannot cope with a no-growth "economy"; it seems
equally fair to say that contemporary social policy has
difficulty coping with a no-growth economy. The problem of
maintaining job-satisfaction, of motivating productivity, of
sustaining personal growth over a long career, of retraining
the 40-plus -- these are all central to a long-term body of
literature that has grown as our lives have grown longer and
as our institutions have grown larger, employing greater
portions of our work force. The problems of economic equity
and physical working environment have largely been resolved
over the past half-century. Today, the emphasis is on the
social working environment, and there has been a growing

amount of institutional experimentation and investment in
"T-groups," participative management, job enrichment, flex-
time, continuing education, etc. It would appear, however,
that such programs <u>conducted for people in organizational
settings</u> do not long involve participant interest, except
for the relatively brief periods during which there are
ongoing potentials for increasing rewards, or during which
there can be a sense of progress toward the mastery of a
skill or area of knowledge (Bandura (<u>73</u>)).

How can we begin to address the problem of socio-
economic stagflation? First, as far as the economic
aspect is concerned, it is clear that we need a much
better perspective on the long-term performance of the
entire system rather than focusing on a limited number
of short-term, high-volume cash flows. Only a comprehensive
view, for example, can provide us with an adequate understanding of how the costs of our formal social services
and the promise of their universal availability have been
loaded onto our future, and what these expectations mean
in terms of the commitments of our common resources. An
expanded perception of our economic system would also
direct us to a much better understanding of the household's
role in our economy.

Since around the turn of the 20th century, Burns has
determined that the capital investment rates in the household sector of the economy have been higher than the rates
for capital formation in the private sector or in government,
with the annual volume of household capital investment
surpassing that for industrial development in 1958 (<u>74</u>). If
we use Burn's interpretive logic, current Commerce Department statistics suggest that households control slightly over
3/8 of our total national assets, while private production
and services control roughly 1/3, government 1/4, and
agriculture less than 1/10 (<u>75</u>).

What is the meaning of this remarkable propensity for
Americans to invest in their households? Does it merely
reflect increasing personal consumption resulting from long-
term growth in productivity and prosperity? Or does it
result from some collective perception of expected utility?
How much household investment is intended to enhance the
investor's productivity or efficiency, to save energy or
time, to produce additional income, to develop human potential, or to provide greater collective security? How good
are the family's returns on its capital investments, and
are they better or worse than those of the market institutions or the government? Because economic policy does not
perceive the household as a significant productive unit, we

do not measure the costs or efficiencies of its production; its expenditures are commonly viewed as "sinks" in the economic system -- "consumption" and "leisure" -- an "excess" of which may be viewed as self-indulgent, or as detrimental to economic growth and development because it robs industry of venture capital (Roberts (76)).

But, while our economic policy does not view the household as a productive unit, our social policy is fundamentally concerned with the household's products. We support the household's nurturance and development of its human output through A.F.D.C. and student loan programs, etc. When households fail to develop sufficiently enculturated offspring, social policy must deal with the conséquences -- cognitive disfunctions, dependency mentality, juvenile delinquency, functionally non-competent individuals, etc. -- through institutional programs whose costs pose problems for economic policy. Because it perceives the household solely as an economic sink, and not as an economic source, economic policy can generally only deal with these problems as being requirements of social policy, and the results of its failures. Until we have a much more comprehensive understanding of how -- and how much -- we each contribute to, and take from the economy, and how we each are employing our respective resources to perform various tasks, we will be ill-equipped to frame a socially rational economic policy.

Similarly, just as we need a much better sense of our economic mutuality, we need a much better sense of our social mutuality. We need to understand and appreciate not merely the ways by which people are productive in terms of economic markets or job status, but also in terms that can be related to the entire social enterprise. Individuals and groups of individuals must be given a means to understand how their day-to-day activities and their ongoing lives may be assessed not only in terms of personal satisfaction, but also in terms of the mutual satisfaction of the larger community and its members. For example, in an expanding, labor-intensive economy, a mutually beneficial relationship between household and society may well have entailed family production of a large number of offspring imbued with expectations of attractive material rewards and security to be derived from a modicum of basic, childhood schooling followed by life-long participation in some simple if arduous tasks.

But, given current labor markets and evolving economic development patterns, we would suspect that the foregoing model constitutes a less mutually beneficial relationship between families and society than it once did. Automation and the export of industrial work have diminished the economy's

utility for large domestic pools of semi-skilled labor. At
the same time, the shift of economic activity toward knowledge work and problem-solving requires much greater training
and sophistication on the part of the workers that are required. Thus, the economy needs a proportionally smaller,
better educated labor force. Many households appear to have
comprehended this and have been sending fewer, but more
highly trained entrants into the labor market.

The foregoing depiction of a mutually beneficial interaction between households and the larger society may be
fairly self-evident, but many are not. The evidence suggests
(Vaillant (77), Rappoport (78)), for example, that there is
an extremely high correlation between marital success and
measures of career achievement, individual mental and
physical health, and other positive social indicators. Just
as our failure to appreciate the household's economic productivity leads us to ignore the family's contribution to
overall social performance, so too our failure to appreciate
the social productivity of the household and other primary
support networks leads us to ignore their contributions to
economic performance, and bars us from framing an economically rational social policy.

Social Policy and Cultural Sterility

The foregoing discussion was directed at demonstrating
some of the links between economic stagflation and a social
policy which focuses on the institutional delivery of
services to a limited number of qualified social forms. Now,
let us turn to a second major problem of contemporary social
policy -- its tendency to promote political conflict, and
cultural monolithicism and sterility. The institutional
drive for "stylistic standards" by which to determine eligibility for common resources distributed via social policies
inherently produces conflicts over who -- or what -- shall be
included in, or excluded from, society's largesse. Shall
public funds be used to pay for or subsidize abortions?
Shall we pay institutions to care for the elderly, but not
pay households to do so? Shall couples living together
without benefit of wedlock receive welfare? Shall homo-
sexuals be guaranteed public protection of their rights
to employment, housing or credit?

So long as social policy is focused primarily upon
social forms rather than social performance, it will in-
evitably generate -- and suffer from -- such political conflicts. Further, as various groups in society find their
values, behavioral styles and institutional forms disadvantaged,
or excluded by social policy, they seek to achieve autonomy

from such policies, and freedom from the imposition of norms
that are not their own or that they do not perceive to be
utile. This pursuit of cultural/stylistic integrity, in turn,
provokes another class of political conflicts -- e.g., "save
the neighborhood school," "keep development out," dual-
language schooling, regional factionalism, (e.g., Ecotopia)
and cultural separatism (e.g., independence movements by
Basques, Bretons, Kurds, Quebeccoise, Waloons, Mollucans,
Khazaks, etc.).

In summarizing what we have learned from cross-cultural
surveys, Narroll noted that more powerful societies tend to
share the following fundamental characteristics: they are
run by exploitative elites through complex, highly specialized structures; further, ruling elites maintain their
positions partially by promoting conflict between ethnic
subgroups possessing different values (79). Such strategies
unavoidably make ethnicity and fertility both political
issues and political instruments. Within recent years, for
example, the French Canadians -- who had been predicting
that they would ultimately control their nation politically by
outbreeding the Anglo's -- discovered that their fertility
had dropped below that of their non-French countrymen
(de Lestapis (80)). Further, they found that a substantial
fraction of the Franco's were moving out of their home province, while the bulk of those moving into the province were
retaining Anglo cultural and behavioral styles, and that in
less than two generations -- 30 years -- the French would
lose political control of Quebec.

In response to the foregoing perceptions, the French
Canadians concluded that, to survive as a culture, they would
have to radically change government policy to forcefully
convert the Anglo's in their midst while they still retained
political control.

These same issues loom implicitly in the disparate birth
rates of white and black Americans, and in the explosive
growth of the Spanish-speaking population in the U.S. How
can the institutional instruments of our current social
policy rationally accommodate the differing values and life-
styles of these ethnic communities? And if it cannot, what
will be the consequences? If, for example, through political
compromise and court decisions, our social services and
public institutions are made bi-lingual -- like Canada,
Belgium, South Africa -- who will bear the very substantial
economic costs, and what benefits or detriments will the
society as a whole experience? If, on the other hand, social
policy rejects demands for official bi-lingualism, what will
be the cultural and political ramifications; what is the

potential for cultural conflict and separatism in America?
We instinctively feel uncomfortable with either alternative,
but it is unclear that the current mode of social policy-
making can ultimately avoid this choice or others like it.

In fact, the rise of so-called "single-issue" politics
may be directly attributed to the nature of our present
social policy. Political and social events of the past two
decades have demonstrated proven methods by which like-minded
individuals may collaborate in order to influence the
policies of corporate and governmental mega-institutions. As
a society, we have seen -- and learned -- the utility of
political mobilization and legal initiative, both collective
behavioral styles that are in consonance with the bulk of our
normative social values. Today, a single session of Congress
or sitting of the Supreme Court can effect dozens of major
adjustments in the entitlements of millions of Americans.
But even when "resolved" by one arm of government or another,
such conflicts do not go away, because the people involved
do not go away.

In sum, social policy which comprehends only a limited
range of social forms and behaviors unavoidably engenders
conflict; worse, it tends to constantly focus our attention
on the differences among us rather than our commonalities and
agreements. It forces us to be contentious -- litigious --
with one another. Holloway and Hornstein have shown in
experiments that individuals exposed to negative news broad-
casts subsequently exhibit substantially diminished altruistic behavior (81). There is no reason to believe that
this same dynamic does not apply to society as a whole, nor
to believe that continuous media reporting of conflicts among
ourselves is not serving to erode the altruistic base of our
society.

Altruism and Competition: Basis for Common Enterprise

How can we apply some process of thought to resolving
situations in which reasonable people disagree, perhaps on
the basis of deeply held beliefs? To begin with, let us
accept the proposition -- advanced earlier -- that any life-
style, family structure or mode of child-rearing represents
a particular way of handling pertinent circumstances -- of
coping with reality. Since people and their circumstances
differ widely throughout society, it is reasonable to assume
that the universe of optimal behavior will be subject to some
variance. If every individual were able to identify and
adopt the optimal primary group arrangement and career/life
development pattern for his or her particular needs and
abilities, we may also assume that both society as a whole

and its individual members would benefit from the resulting
increased productivity and collective mental health. But how
might we achieve such a happy state of affairs?

Certainly, we would need to create some sort of process
for providing individuals with the means to identify suitable
life strategies. But we would also need to demonstrate
sufficient mutual altruism to accept the diversity of life-
styles that would be engendered by such a process.

Altruism is the basis of family life, and ultimately, of
society itself. Altruistic behavior is widely seen in animal
societies in the nurturance of young, protection of the weak,
succor of the sick or wounded, sharing of food, etc. At the
same time, it is clear that group arrangements entail some
very significant disfunctions for individual group members,
the chief among which is competition for scarce resources
(Anderson (82)). Other detrimental aspects of group living
include problems of organization and coordination -- i.e.,
Boulding's "palaver" -- (83) plus heightened visibility to
predators and the contagion of negative elements (disease,
pessimism, rumors, etc.). The questions, then, must be,
given such detrimental aspects, why do individuals enter into
such arrangements? What is the basis of altruistic behavior?

Collective altruism arises in circumstances under which
two or more individuals can each gain greater benefit by
acting together than they can by acting separately. Rudimentary examples of this are group defense and pack hunting.
Once groups coalesce for specific mutual benefit, it appears
that the dynamics of group interaction promote individual
effectiveness. Smith shows mathematically that competitors
in the same stable area will tend to develop non-conflicting
specialties (84). Conversley, Antonovics shows that the
greater the similarity between individuals, the stronger the
competition (85). Further, competition can be moderated, as
Boulding has noted, by signalling the likely outcome of conflict in advance (86). Similarly, signalling (communication)
can speed and increase mutual exploitation of situations
through more rapid discovery and coordination; additional
adaptation and specialization can occur based upon this
communication, further enhancing individual and collective
performance.

Where altruistic collaboration increases the immediate
gain of each participant, the utility of such behavior is
apparent. The only way for altruism to thrive as a norm,
however, is among other altruists in relatively bounded
situations; otherwise, scarce resources will be dissipated.
The easiest way to restrict benefits to other altruists is by

signalling -- by exchanging mutual commitments and expectations. But within such altruistic communities or networks,
there is still the question of helping others against self-
interest. Here, both giving and taking among mutual altruists also appear to be facilitated by communication, in the
form of collective accounting which transcends individual
resources and immediate personal gain, to acknowledge common
resources and to reward both individual and collective investments over time. Thus, investing in others at the
expense of one's own limited time and resources (e.g., longer
nurturance of offspring), is promoted when such expenditures
are perceived to be ultimately more rewarding both to the
investor and to the community as a whole than the immediate
personal benefits foregone. Such altruistic accounting
underlies the fundamental legitimacy of any tax system.

Thus, it would appear that altruism in social arrangements of whatever scale is based upon some calculus by which
individual needs, desires or ideals, etc., may be perceived
as most effectively realized through collaboration with
others. This calculus operates on the basis of information
about pertinent environments and the probable outcomes of
differing strategies. By communicating with one another, the
participants in a collaborative endeavor can increase both
their knowledge of the environment and of the probable consequences of alternative actions or investments. Wiens
points out that, partly because of limitations in conveying
learning genetically, there is very considerable fluctuation
in the "information environs" of lower order animals which
largely self-limits learning -- as a result, effective
altruistic behavior must be relearned each generation and
social evolution can move no further forward (87).

Human societies, however, are different. While many
lower animals learn their behaviors from their elders and
pass down a rudimentary culture, the preponderance of their
behavior is genetically determined. Humans are the first
animals to make culture the dominant determiner of their
behavior. Although some variation in human behavior is
passed on through genetic channels (e.g., impacts on vari-
ances in I.Q. potential, etc.), this influence is small compared with the degree to which culture shapes human behavior
and styles, including our attitudes toward, and our utilities
for, altruistic behavior. Further, through this enculturation process, the bulk of which takes place within the
household/friendship network, the cultural perception of
altruism evolves in accordance to each succeeding generation's experience. And, it is at this critical juncture
that cultural modernization has so altered the context of
social adaptation that it may have seriously reduced its

effectiveness. It is also at this juncture that social
policy may best serve to restore that effectiveness.

Evolving Perceptions of the Common Enterprise

Prior to industrialization and modernization, the
social context for most individuals was generally quite
simple, and encompassed a relatively limited space or geographic area. Within such a context, household/friendship
networks provided an adequate experience base for fairly
depicting the universe of social and economic utilities and
behavioral styles, and the dynamics which governed their
interaction. The past several generations have altered and
perhaps weakened our family/friendship networks. But more
importantly, as society has grown in size, complexity and
diversity, it is no longer possible for network members to
experience -- first-hand -- the bulk of our social and economic arrangements, or the implications of these arrangements
for adjusting our cultural images of utilitarian behavior.
Absent such experience, enculturation may still communicate
a high normative value for altruism as an ideal, but it is
less able to convey contemporary images of effective altruistic behavior. Further, the flow of negative news regarding
conflict among individual and collective members of our
national enterprise may well be diminishing the normative
value for altruism as well.

Given the real possibility that our principal mechanisms
of enculturation may be communicating diminished utilities
for altruistic behavior, and further given the uncertainties
posed by the current fundamental changes in our social and
economic contexts, the current tendency toward single, self-
sufficient life styles may simply reflect the natural
adoption of what is perceived by many to be the most utilitarian mode of functioning. If this is the case, how may
social policy legitimately intervene to alter these perceptions and promote more altruistic arrangements? Certainly
not by providing artificial incentives for particular forms
of behavior (e.g., elimination of the so-called "marriage
tax") or through regulation (e.g., making divorce or
abortions harder to obtain); this will only provoke more
conflict. Rather, the nature of the process for social
adaptation and cultural evolution presented in this paper
suggests very strongly that it is the responsibility of
social policy to do for society what society can not do for
itself; it must provide much more information about our
social and economic mutuality, and the nature and effectiveness of our individual and collective behaviors.

Our sprawling, multi-ethnic, multi-specialized world is

easily perceived as a confusing, tumultuous crowd of pervasive conflicts and irrational differences. Through
expanded monitoring and reporting, the public sector can
improve our understanding of what is going on in society, and
of the probable consequences of alternative life-style
choices and institutional arrangements.

For example, if we comprehend families merely to be the
normative cultural form for cohabitation, breeding, and
child-rearing, we ignore their other important social and
economic functions, and thereby discount the family's importance to society as a whole. Thus, the commonly experienced
detriments of familial collaboration may be seen by many as
outweighing its perceived personal and social benefits, which
are neither so immediate or apparent as the detriments. But,
if social policy were to generate a more comprehensive image
of how familial and other life-styles impact upon individual
performance and overall economic productivity, then individual choices among life styles would be made more rational.

Recent significant reductions (from 15-85%) (88) in
death rates associated with some forms of heart disease,
hypertension, cerebro-vascular disease, diabetes and arterio-
scelrosis have been directly laid by medical experts to
improved diet and health regimes that have been voluntarily
adopted by large numbers of Americans on the basis of published reports reflecting scientific findings regarding
detrimental or beneficial patterns of behavior. It does not
strain credulity to believe that this same dynamic would
operate in response to improved general knowledge regarding
the most effective prophylaxis or cure for social disfunctions. Surely this very dynamic is reflected in the
growing adoption of health maintenance organization (HMO's)
throughout our society. Based upon empirical evidence of the
enormous social and economic productivity of preventative
medicine, we are presently moving to institutionalize this
mode of health delivery whose practical utility had already
been demonstrated by the voluntary -- and initially experimental -- adoption of innovative attitudinal and behavioral
health styles. The adoption of consciously healthful
behavior at the primary group level reflects efforts by
individuals and households to maximize their investments
towards survival and prosperity. The adoption of preventative health care by the institutional sector reflects
parallel efforts to maximize the productivity of our common
resources.

Informing Personal Development and Social Policy

The provision of more and better socio-economic

performance indicators will not, by itself, permit the sort
of evolution we are experiencing in our health policy and
health styles. Diet and personal health habits are largely
left to free choice in our society, State and Federal regulations and general economic considerations notwithstanding.
Thus, evolutionary adoption of innovative health habits has
largely been left unfettered. Our social forms, on the other
hand, are substantially limited, by law and by convention,
which make exploration in these areas as difficult as housing
innovation under building codes based upon material or design
specifications rather than upon performance specifications.
Just because post and lintel construction has worked since
the dawn of history, and just because it can be seen
functioning in current construction, does not mean that we
all gain from making it the only acceptable manner of construction. The ethic of administration should be exploration,
and not extrapolation.

Thus, in addition to providing considerably more
comprehensive knowledge about the performance of our diverse
primary group forms and about their relative contributions to
the overall national enterprise, social policy must also
permit -- if not encourage -- the adoption of new primary
group forms, much in the same way that nation encouraged
exploration and economic entrepreneurship when our frontiers
were territorial or commercial. Through expanded monitoring
of life-style performance indicators, the effectiveness of
various forms of social collaboration in different contexts
and for different tasks can be assessed and made known to
society as a whole. With such information, individuals can
identify effective social and economic performances which
corrolate with their normative values and behavioral styles,
and assimilate this knowledge into their understanding of
future utilitarian behavior. This, in turn, can be expected
to influence their life-style choices, and the values and
expectations which they pass on to their off-spring.

Having thus facilitated the rationalization of social
adaptation, social policy could scarcely seek to bar that
adaptive process from working: nor should it try! Rather,
it should seek to facilitate the process by making it orderly,
equitable, and responsible, in the same manner that economic
policy has a legitimate concern for preventing excesses and
abuses of the marketplace. At the very minimum, then, there
would need to be some rules by which new social arrangements
might formally establish, amend, or dis-establish themselves.
But the most important function of government in enabling the
effectiveness of social adaptation must be to provide for
the increased flow of information by which we may assess
the performance of differing forms of family/friendship

collaborations.

It is not very useful, for example, for demographics to
tell us that median household income is $17,000 per annum.
We must know the median income of single households, couples,
2 and 3 generation families, group marriages, communes, etc.,
as these groups function over time. We also need to know per
capita energy consumption, mental and physical health rates,
transiency, expenditure patterns and capital formation,
public aid and other subsidies received, scholastic and
career performance, professional and community tasks and
roles, etc., for each of the entire array of primary groups.

Over time, these data will begin to reveal differing
performance patterns for different household arrangements;
those arrangements reflecting superlative performances will
become models for effective human collaboration, to be
emulated both for their benefits to the individual members
and to society at large. Around the pursuit of optimum life
styles, a social market place could evolve, including
mechanisms for recruiting and developing people (children
and adults) who could vote with their feet (competition) and
carry some form of development credits and pension rights
with them.

Clearly, such a process would require an enormous amount
of record-keeping and reporting. Fortunately, the rapidly
expanding capacities of electronic information technology
have timely appeared to provide the facile capability to
record and report such masses of data, often as a by-product
of action. Current estimates of the projected growth of the
popular info-com market suggests that half of all U.S.
households will possess home computers and be linked to at
least one inter-active communications network within the
next decade. This voluntary investment will provide households with the infra-structure for recording and reporting
on their performances. Further, the new communications
networks will provide considerable geographic reach in establishing and maintaining personal networks throughout the
nation and the world. In our large, highly-transient society,
this capacity to sustain family/friendship collaborations
over distances must be regarded to be as fundamental a
feature of our lives as the right to assembly. Social policy
must foster such technologies as a prime requirement for
increasing inter-personal "signalling" and mutual altruism.

Social Evolution and Social Insurance

It is in the interests of the community not to isolate
its members from each other -- not to force them back into

small house-holes where their exposure to altruistic behavior
is limited at best. Citizens have not only the right, but
the responsibility for developing their own values and views,
and for experiencing the tangible results in their daily
lives. This is the communiversity, which rounds out the
basic personal development provided by the "household school,"
as discussed by Dr. Warnat earlier in this volume. Only by
acting upon our beliefs can we dismiss immature dreams and
develop the realistic judgements upon which the democratic
process relies for its effectiveness. Improved social
accounting can only facilitate this life-long learning and
development, by providing us with much better understandings
of the full array of social arrangements, their effectiveness
in fulfilling their member's needs and potentials, and their
contributions to the larger community.

Informed by these understandings, individuals and groups
in our society will be able to make better predictions
concerning the probable outcomes arising from different
behaviors and investments, thereby speeding their evolution
toward productive participation in society. The very process
of measuring one's own performance -- or that of one's primary
group -- against other social forms, will increase one's
sense of real participation in the whole, and of contributing
meaningfully to our mutual altruism.

The outputs of improved social accounting would also
inform social policy. There is no free lunch: society has
many valid interests but limited resources. The life
earnings of several responsible citizens may be eaten up
handling the results of one person's drug experiments or
botched child rearing. What risks can society afford to
take? Similarly, what risks can society afford to have its
citizens take? If we are to have both personal growth and
societal health, the terms of our collective social insurance
can involve neither a blank check nor protective custody. A
social accounting system would provide us not only with
models for effective human collaboration and social altruism;
it would also provide us with models of life-styles which are
socially or economically disfunctional. In particular, it
would reveal to us the patterns of behavior which result in
net losses to our common resource base. And, where voluntary
life-style adaptations toward socially responsible behavior
do not occur, social policy may use such information to
legitimately intervene in the process to provide the incentives or decrements to encourage such behavior. In this
context, the debate over particular social forms or behaviors
would focus not merely on their perceived sanctity or
morality, but also upon their larger role in our social and
economic mutuality.

Given a relatively comprehensive system of social
accounting and public reporting, social policy conflicts
should ultimately be minimized. There appear to be some deep
universal strategies for handling the paradoxes of life; even
the lower animal forms converge on such strategies in simpler
situations. Individuals, families and other human groupings
work via strategies developed through observation, experience
and practice. The results of such experiments and explora-
tions should be shared with society as elements of a common
science. The new information technologies, given support by
the larger society, offer reasonable hope of our being able
to extract many of the elements of this common science and
making them available to all.

Today, we are undergoing major transformations in our
population structure, and in our economic and technological
bases, all of which are creating a rather different milieu
from the one by which our current intuitions have been
shaped. At the same time, a large portion of our population
are caught in personal situations which do not permit them to
effectually participate in the action, although they may
vividly see, and actively seek opportunities to contribute to
the larger community in some meaningful way. We are "buying
off" most of these individuals with meaningless roles (e.g.,
dependency, salary serfdom, forced retirement, welfare, etc.)
which merely serves to put them in a sort of time capsule,
with a window on the excitement. The support of these
passively encapsulated millions not only fosters stagflation,
but will predictably destroy the entire system if extra-
polated on the basis of current trends. Even if the economic
burden of our dependents does not crush us, the weakening of
the nation's altruistic base, exacerbated by our removal of
millions of Americans from access to opportunities for
meaningful participation and collaboration, can only result
in the fragmentation and deterioration of society.

It should be the primary task of social policy to
provide the citizenry with some overall sense of what is
going on in society, and of how individuals and groups may
effectively participate in the action with some reasonable
expectation of meaningful rewards for both the participants
and society at large. Concurrently, social policy must
provide the legal and communications infrastructure to
facilitate the adoption of collaborative arrangements which
people believe merit their commitment. Finally, social
policy must eschew direct intervention in the resulting
dynamics except where specific arrangements or behaviors can
be demonstrated to result in increased dependency upon the
larger society, and in net losses to our common resources.
Only in this manner can society rationally assimilate the

paradoxes of modern complexity and promote the productivity
of mutual altruism at all levels of the national community.

References

1. E. Durkheim, Le Suicide, (Paris, 1897)
    ed. G. Simpson (Free Press, N.Y., 1951)
    Durkheim examined modern social forms as sources of
    meaning, and rejects the family, state, religion and
    local community. He hypothesizes that occupational
    groups (whose sense of meaning is based on their
    specializations for productivity) would provide meaning.
    To some degree such occupation groupings are found
    naturally in different city neighborhoods with dif-
    ferentiations based on economics and some on aesthetics.
    My discussion of these differentiating factors was
    recorded by the AAAS and is available on their tapes of
    the 1978 session "Neighborhoods and Cities;" an
    extension of these remarks is in preparation.

2. E. Boulding, The Underside of History.
    (Westview Press, Boulder, Colorado, 1977)

3. P. Aries, His most recent views in English are in a
    review and precis of L. Stone's The Family, Sex, and
    Marriage in England 1500-1600 in American History
    Review 1978, 83, p. 1221-1224. But also see Aries,
    Centuries of Childhood: A Social History of the Family,
    (A. A. Knopf, N.Y., N.Y., 1965). A critique of Aries'
    work may be found in D. Hunt, Parents and Children in
    History: Psychology of Family in Early Modern Europe,
    (Basic Books, N.Y., N.Y., 1970).

4. P. Laslett, Household and Family in Past Time,
    (Cambridge University Press, Cambridge, Mass., 1972).

5. J. F. Kett, Rites of Passage, Adolescence in America
    1790 - Present, (Basic Books, N.Y., N.Y., 1977).

6. Laslett, Op. Cit. (4). For another example of a
    convergence of family practice despite divergent
    ideology, see J. W. Cole, "Inheritance Processes and
    their Social Consequences," Sociologia; revista di
    studi sociali, 4, p. 133-146.

7. E. O. Wilson, Sociobiology, Harvard Press, Cambridge,
    Mass., 1975).

8. P. Campanella, "Temporal Leks As A Mating System in a Temperate Zone Dragonfly," Behavior, 1973, 51.

9. L. Minturn and W. W. Lambert, Mothers of 6 Cultures: Antecedents of Child-Rearing, Wiley, N.Y., N.Y., 1964.

10. J. Sawyer and R. A. Levine, "Cultural Dimensions: A Factor Analysis of the World Ethnographic Sample" American Anthropologist, 1968, 4, p. 708-731.

11. H. Barry III., L. Josephson, D. Lauer, and C. Marshall, "Traits Inculcated in Childhood; Cross-Cultural Codes 5," Ethnology, 1969, 15, p. 83-114.

12. B. B. Whiting and J. W. M. Whiting, Childhood in Six Cultures: A Psycho-Cultural Survey (Harvard Press, Cambridge, Mass., 1976).

13. Barry, et. al., 1969, Op. Cit., (11).

14. N. Miller, "American Universities Field Staff," 1975, Ann Arbor, Michigan.

15. J. Kagan, "The Child in the Family," Daedalus, 1977, 106, 2, p. 33-56.

16. For a general introduction see B. Bernstein, Social Linguistics, A Course Module from the Open University of Great Britain, 1975. See also E. T. Higgins "Social Class Differences in Verbal Communicative Accuracy," Psychological Bulletin, 1976, 83, p. 695-714.

17. A. Astin, Who Goes Where to College, (Science Research Associates, Chicago, 1975).

18. Sawyer and Levine, 1968, Op. Cit., (10).

19. R. M. Kantor, Men and Women in Corporations, (Basic Books, N.Y., 1977).

20. M. D. Cohen and J. G. March, Leadership and Ambiguity (McGraw Hill, N.Y., N.Y., 1977).

21. E. Brunswick, "Psychoanalysis and Personality Research," Abnormal and Social Psychology, 35, p. 76-197. See also Tolman and Brunswick, Op. Cit., (9).

22. H. C. Triandis, The Analysis of Subjective Culture, (Wiley-Interscience, N.Y., N.Y., 1972).

23. A. I. Inkeles and D. H. Smith, Becoming Modern,
     (Harvard University Press, Cambridge, Mass., 1975).

24. H. A. Witkin and D. R. Goodenough, "Field Independence
     and Interpersonal Behavior," Psychological Bulletin,
     1977, 89, 4, p. 661-689. A larger review and perspective
     of this field is given in Journal of Cross-Cultural
     Psychology, 1975, 6, p. 4-87.

25. H. Zuckerman, address to the American Association for
     the Advancement of Science, 1971.

26. R. Scribner and S. Coe, "Cross Cultural Factors in
     Education," Science, 1975.

27. F. E. Emory, E. L. Trist, Towards a Social Ecology
     (Plenum Publishing, N.Y., N.Y., 1975).

28. H. Simon, Models of Man, (Wiley, New York, 1957),
     "Rational Choice and the Structure of the Environment,"
     Psychological Review, 63, p. 129-138.

29. Hare, The Handbook of Small Group Research, (The Free
     Press, N.Y., N.Y., 1976).

30. Bernstein, 1975, Op. Cit., (16).

31. A. Lomax, a progress report made to the staff, National
     Science Foundation, January, 1978.

32. Scribner and Coe, 1975, Op. Cit., (26).

33. R. M. Kantor, 1977, Op. Cit.

34. A. Lomax, "Evolutionary Taxonomy of Culture," Science,
     1975, 177, p. 228-239.

35. R. M. Kantor, 1977, Op. Cit., (19).

36. H. C. Triandis, 1972, Op. Cit., (22).

37. R. Cattell, Abilities: Their Structure, Growth and
     Action, (Houghton Mifflin, Boston, 1971).

38. P. Sorokin, Social and Cultural Dynamics, (Beckminster
     Press, N.Y., N.Y., 1939).

39. C. Morris, Signification and Significance, (M.I.T.
     Press, Cambridge, Mass., 1954).

40. C. Arensburg, Preprint and Personal Communication, 1975.
Also see "Culture as Behavior: Structure and Emergence,"
Annual Review of Anthropology, Vol. 1, (Annual Reviews,
Inc., Palo Alto, California, 1972).

41. A. Toynbee, "Higher Religious and Psychological Types,"
A Study of History, Vol. 7B, (Oxford University Press,
1954).

42. E. Neumann, The Origins and History of Consciousness
(Princeton University Press, Princeton, N.J., 1954).

43. N. Frye, Anatomy of Criticism, (Princeton University
Press, Princeton, N.J., 1957).

44. I. T. Mitoff and R. H. Kilmann, Technology Forecasting
and Social Change, 1976, 8, 2, p. 163-174.

45. T. Parsons, Systems of Modern Societies, (Prentice-Hall
Inc., Engelwood Cliffs, N.J., 1971).

46. Wish and Wish, The Journal of Personality and Social
Psychology, 1976, 33.

47. H. C. Triandis, 1972, Op. Cit., (22).

48. H. J. Bremmerman, "Optimization through Evolution and
Recombination," in Self-Organizing Systems - 1962.

49. For an introductory discussion of this work see
C. Cherry, On Human Communications, 2nd edition,
(MIT Press, Cambridge, Mass., 1977).

50. G. A. Miller, "The Magic Number Seven, Plus or Minus
Two" Some Limits on our Capacity for Processing Information," Psychological Review, 63, 2, p. 81-96.

51. J. H. Conway, On Numbers and Games, (Academic Press,
N. Y., N.Y., 1976).

52. T. G. Room, A Background - Natural, Synthetic and
Algebraic - to Geometry, (Cambridge University Press,
Cambridge, Mass., 1967).

53. M. Mead, interview "Coming of Age on Earth," The New
Age, 1977, 2, 12, p. 22.

54. Parsons, 1972, Op. Cit., (45).

55. A. Lomax, "Appeal for Cultural Equity: When Cultures Clash," Journal of Communications, 1977, 27.

56. S. Duncan Jr., D. W. Fiske, Face to Face Interaction Research Methods, Theory (L. Erlbaum, Hillside, N.J. associate publishers: distributed by Wiley, 1977).

57. R. L. Birdwhistle, Kinesics and Context, (University of Pennsylvania Press, Philadelphia, Pa., 1970).

58. J. A. Brittan, The Inheritance of Economic Status and Inheritance and the Inequality of Material Wealth, (Brookings Institution, Washington, D.C., 1977).

59. J. Jacobs, The Life and Death of Great American Cities, (Pantheon, N.Y., N.Y., 1962) and The Economy of Cities, (Vintage, N.Y., N.Y., 1970).

60. A. Toynbee, 1954, Op. Cit., (41).

61. A. Astin, Four Critical Years, (Josey-Bass, San Francisco, 1977).

62. K. Arrow, "The Economic Implications of Learning by Doing," Review of Economic Studies, June, 1962, p. 155-173.

63. J. Kagan, 1977, Op. Cit., (15).

64. Bernstein, 1975, Op. Cit.

65. W. E. Barron, and C. R. Kelso, Adult Functional Competency, Report Submitted to the Adult Education Division, U.S. Office of Education, March, 1975.

66. K. V. Flannery, "The Cultural Evolution of Civilization," The Annual Review of Ecology and Systematics, 5, p. 399-426, (Annual Reviews Inc., Palo Alto, Ca., 1972).

67. J. A. Wiens, "On Competition and Variable Environments," American Scientist, 1978, 66, p. 590.

68. P. Burger, B. Burger, D. Kelner, The Homeless Mind: Modernity and Consciousness, (Random House, N.Y., N.Y., 1973).

69. R. M. Maroney, The Family and the State: Considerations for Social Policy, (Longman, London, 1977).

70. Statistical Abstract of the United States, 1977, Table 3.

71. M. Olken, "Stagflation," The Brooking Bulletins, 14, 3, p. 1-7.

72. National Cross-sections interviewed by the Survey Research Center, University of Michigan, 1972.

73. A. Bandura, "Cognitive Processes Mediating Behavioral Change," Journal of Personality and Social Psychology, 35, 3.

74. R. Narroll, "What We Have Learned from Cross-Cultural Surveys?" American Anthropologist, 1970, 72, 6, p. 83-114.

75. Statistical Abstract of the United States, 1977, Tables 750-758.

76. P. C. Roberts, "The Tax Brake," The Wall Street Journal, January 11, 1979.

77. G. E. Vaillant, Adaption to Life, (Little, Brown & Co., 1977).

78. Rappoport, 1978, Op. Cit.

79. Narroll, Op. Cit.

80. R. P. S. de Lestapis, "The Fertility Crisis in Quebec," p. 6-11, Population Issues in Canada, ed. C. F. Grindstaff et. al. (Holt, Rinehart & Wilson, 1971). This is a translation of work done for The Council on French Life in America in 1967.

81. S. M. Holloway and H. A. Hornstein, "How Good News Makes Us Good," Psychology Today, 1976, 10, 6, p. 76-78.

82. R. D. Anderson, "The Evolution of Social Behavior," The Review of Ecology and Systematics, p. 325-384, (Annual Reviews, Inc., Palo Alto, Ca., 1974).

83. K. E. Boulding, Conflict and Defense: A General Theory, (Harper & Row, N.Y., N.Y., 1962).

84. M. Smith, "Evolution and the Theory of Games," American Scientist, 1976, 64, p. 41.

85. J. Antonovics, "The Effects of a Heterogeneous Environment on the Genetics of Natural Populations," American Scientist, 1971, 59, p. 593-599.

86. Boulding, 1962, Op. Cit., (82).

87.   Wiens, 1978, Op. Cit., (<u>67</u>).

88.   <u>Statistical Abstract of the United States</u>, 1977,
      Table 104.

6

The Family
An Appropriate Technology
for America's Third Century

David P. Snyder

When E. F. Schumacher first ennunciated the idea of "appropriate technology," (1) the concept was thought of almost exclusively in terms of the applied uses of hard scientific knowledge, principally in the less developed nations. Over the years, the number of adherents to Schumacher's philosophy have grown, and an increasing portion of those adherents have become concerned with the uses of intermediate physical technologies in the developed, industrial nations as well. At the same time, other scholars and analysts have begun to explore the implications of Schumacher's concepts for the social technologies--for socio-economic processes and institutions.

It is inevitable that, as the concept of "appropriate technology" assumes paradigmatic scope and breadth, we must ultimately come to a working understanding of the family and familiar groups as social and economic technologies that are most appropriate for certain tasks within our community. In many societies today, and in our own society within living memory, the family has served as a very powerful technology, providing a broad array of social and economic goods and services. During the past century, higher social technologies have been developed in order to provide some of the services traditionally produced by the more fundamental family technology--e.g., social security, workman's compensation, unemployment benefits, convalescent and child care, educational loans, sex education, health insurance, etc. Throughout this same period, the household has increasingly been superceded as a commercial production technology, a trend that first began with the rise of industrialism.

In spite of the family's diminishing functional obligations, however, Professor Boulding has posited that the household continued to make unique contributions to our society

and our economy, based upon the particular effectiveness and
efficiency of its internal transaction mechanisms. Dr.
Warnat has ascribed to the household singular capacities for
developing and refining its members' emotional and social
effectiveness throughout their lives. Dr. Stack has observed
that the family household is a durable social and economic
form that has demonstrated, through time and across cultural
boundaries, remarkable abilities to optimize its functions by
adapting to the realities of its environment. And, Dr.
Edwards has suggested that the familial group operates in a
remarkable variety of modes to undergird our hierarchy of
social, economic and political institutions by nurturing and
sustaining effective, creative individuals.

In our discussions concerning public policy toward the
family, it seems to me that we should focus upon those functions for which the family institution has a demonstrated
capacity for effective performance, and in particular, upon
those functions which the family appears to perform better
than other known alternatives. Basically, what we must consider is that families and familiar groups may be the most
appropriate institutional forms for providing a number of services that are presently produced by larger-scale social and
economic technologies. For example:

Education. Numerous statistical indicators reflect the
changing nature of our formal educational processes, whereby
increasing numbers of adults are spending more and more time
in a variety of educational pursuits; continuing their learning throughout their lives in order to improve their performance on the job, to qualify for higher positions, to broaden
or change careers, or for a variety of other recreational or
avocational purposes. Thus, we see that learning is indeed
becoming a life-long activity, one for which the school-house-
hold, as Dr. Warnat has described it, would appear to be the
most appropriate base, particularly when given access,
through the burgeoning info-com technologies, to all of the
reference knowledge, specialized counselling and programmed
teaching/testing necessary to meet each individual's learning
needs.

Economic Production. During the past century and a half,
the logistical imperatives of the industrial system of manu-
facturing and the economic efficiencies of specialization and
mass production have combined to strip the family of most of
its commercial production functions. Ironically, this development followed a period when families had served as the
basis for the emergence of mercantilism and the rise of
cities and the middle class throughout Europe. But just as
the family farm gave way to the factory with the shift in the

dominant economic activity from agriculture to industry, the
recent emergence of information as a pre-eminent economic
commodity makes possible a resurging role for small, cooperative units as important commercial producers and entrepre-
neurs. Assuming the continued explosive growth of home computers, computer communications networks, and commercial data
bases, households could serve as producers of a broad range
of specialized knowledges and information, plus networking,
editing and publishing, research, analytical and ideogenetic
services, etc.

Social Security. The large-scale institutional forms of
social security have been regarded as a hallmark of civilized
evolution. And, no doubt, they are! However, in their sys-
temic efforts to most equitably maximize the generalized public good, such institutions encounter diseconomies and com-
plexities to scale which some classify as "dehumanizing."
Such institutions as social security, medicare, unemployment
insurance, workman's compensation, and food stamps, etc.,
were originally designed to apply only to those who needed
them. However, in the egalitarian milieu of the Western nations, these social technologies tend to evolve into universal rights. And, as social, economic and geographic mobility
have dismantled the extended household, the institutional social technologies have naturally expanded to provide the security functions that the evolving nuclear family could less
and less easily fulfill.

Of course, we recognize that there is also an element of
paternalism in the large-scale social technologies; a sense
that the institutional technologies must provide security because the citizen is, in the main, unable or unlikely to do
so. We insure that the citizen (and by extension, his/her
family) put aside something for a rainy day by withholding
health and unemployment insurance premiums from the take-home
pay; taxes, too.

Businesses, on the other hand, are more trusted to manage their own financial fortunes, since they are expected to
behave on the basis of the formalized responsibility that
goes with the legal and economic rituals of being in commerce.
Some years ago, during the rush to establish Community Action
Programs and Head Start Centers at the outbreak of the "War
on Poverty," I was one of several hundred hastily-trained
"community development consultants" who spread out across the
nation to meet and deal with city councils, county clerks,
school superintendents, ministers, and other local leaders
who wished to set up anti-poverty programs of one or another
sort. Budget estimates were picked out of the blue, and in
order to meet the statutory requirement that local agencies

or communities provide at least 10% of the necessary program
resources, hasty dollar value appraisals were made of church
basements, vacant lots, shade trees and hypothetical volun-
teers. On the basis of these estimates, hundreds of millions
of dollars were paid in operating grants, so that people
could be provided with consumer counselling and education, so
preschool children could get hot meals and medical and dental
examinations, and so that parents could pool their efforts to
provide day care for their kids and get paid for it.

All of this was done,--federal funding was provided--so
long as there were designated officers--accountants, lawyers,
and knowledgeable citizens--not just amateur do-gooders,
responsible for the enterprise.

As was observed at the outset of this volume, about one-
half of America's businesses--around 5 million firms--have
adjusted gross incomes of $10,000 or less per annum, while
there are nearly 30 million American families with AGI's in
excess of that amount. If we were to acknowledge the economic and social functions of the family by permitting households to operate as the economic enterprises which they are;
if we were to permit them to be responsible, within some
bounds, for their own security and to invest in their own
educational and productive resources, most families could
cope for themselves. This would remove considerable burden
from a number of presently strained social delivery systems,
by enabling millions of families to collectively take on many
responsibilities for themselves and their individual members
that are currently assigned, through tax transfers and legis-
lated programs, to governmental jurisdictions. By voluntarily taking on the responsibility for managing their own retirement, health, accident, and medical trust funds, tax accounts, educational financing, etc. in conjunction with their
existing resource management responsibilities, families would
regain greater control over their own affairs. The formal
social programs currently responsible for such management
would be freed from handling the accounts of potentially self-
reliant families and their members, and be able to concentrate
on serving those families and individuals who are, as yet,
unable to be self-reliant.

Presently available info-com technologies could provide
family corporations with the information and control--the
"common science," as Dr. Edwards has called it--that would
permit them to function responsibly and effectively to manage
their own resources and expenditures. Electronically equipped
households could also serve as certified repositories for
their members' vital records, and thus serve to protect such
personal data from abuse. Further, the social and economic

implications of large numbers of families which would con-
sistently be able to make "best buy" purchases, to fully utilize all warranty commitments, to claim every benefit permitted by Federal, state and local revenue laws, and to make
effective investments of time and capital--all based upon a
broad range of pertinent economic and ecosystemic inputs--is
patently powerful.

Household incorporation would provide the legal and economic framework which would assure institutional responsibility, so that those families that wished to avail themselves
of the opportunity could be permitted to provide their own
financial security within the context of what the marketplace
of insurance and fiduciary investment could provide. Incorporation has the additional advantage of being a long-stand-
ing, highly flexible socioeconomic technology, which may be
applied to a wide variety of household forms. Thus, the disparate range of family structures which Dr. Stack suggests
has traditionally characterized Western societies could all
be accommodated with equal ease, and without moral biasing.
At the same time, the policy definition problems encountered
by Dr. Allen would also be easily resolved.

If we continue the current trends toward more and larger
social technologies, we cannot help but promote public dependence upon them. After all, that's what they're there for.
Further, as the wealth transfer mechanisms inherent to such
technologies continue to function from one generation to the
next, there will be fewer and fewer of us who will be able to
afford anything but the mega-institutional services that have
been created by our forebears. An alternative road would be
to utilize smaller scale technologies, such as households and
neighborhoods, to deliver some of the necessary goods and services presently provided by large, centralized private and
public sector institutions. If, as Professor Boulding and
Dr. Edwards have both suggested, there is a natural hierarchy
of institutional forms, each with its own specialized mechanisms for economic and social interaction, it is only common
sense for our policy analysis processes to compare our institutions with our social and economic needs, and to match up
those that make the most appropriate and effective partner-
ships.

Note

1. E. F. Schumacher, Small Is Beautiful: Economics As If People Mattered, Harper, New York, 1973.

Schumacher's basic view is that much modern technology and its characteristically large-scale applications are efficient but costly to purchase, operate and maintain. Further, Schumacher maintained that sophisticated, capital-intensive technologies deprive human beings of work and, in general, result in more ecological harm than do less-advanced technologies. Finally, Schumacher believed that complex, centrally managed and controlled technologies force individuals and local communities into far-flung dependency networks over which they have little or no influence, putting them "at the mercy" of potential systems disfunctions against which there are no adequate means of protection.

The most immediate and compelling applications of Professor Schumacher's perceptions have been in the less developed nations, where the concept of "intermediate" or "appropriate" technology has had a strong influence in re-shaping economic development strategies by reducing the previous long-term emphasis on capital-intensive, high technology infrastructure projects (steel mills, tractor factories, airports and highways, etc.) and promoting smaller-scale, labor-intensive projects (small foundries, plow manufacturies serving local markets, water-bound farm-to-market roads, etc.) that are more appropriate to the needs and resources of developing economies.

Professor Schumacher's concepts have had such a powerful global appeal that, in less than five years, Small Is Beautiful has been translated into 15 languages, and organizations for the study and development of intermediate technology have been established in a dozen countries, including the Office of Appropriate Technology of the Agency for International Development and a Federal Center for Appropriate Technologies (Butte, Montana) in the United States.

In the developed nations, popular interest in intermediate technologies has been generated as a result of the energy crisis and concern over the possible environmental decrements which may be associated with some energy-producing technologies. Today, the search for a new energy base in the developed nations finds centralized, capital-intensive high technologies (nuclear fission and fusion, coal gasification, solar satellites, etc.) confronted by a growing interest in and popular support for a host of decentralized, labor-intensive intermediate technologies (passive solar collectors, bio-mass converters, small-scale hydro-turbines, windmills, etc.). Similarly, the supporters of sophisticated, large-scale urban mass transportation technologies (autos and freeways, subways and rapid-rail, etc.) find themselves increasingly pitted against the promoters of bicycles, mopeds and small, self-contained communities.

In the context of social policy, Schumachers's techno-economic precepts have direct antecedents in Emile Durkheim's perception of the need for "intermediary," human-scale institutions to be interposed between the individual members of society and the mega-institutions which dominate policy and decision-making in modern nation states (see the discussion on Durkheim and Marx in the opening pages of Chapter 5 of this book). As opposed to Durkheim's proposals for an entirely new social form it is argued here, in Chapter 6, that the family represents an "intermediate" social technology which is most appropriate for the provision of a variety of social and human development services that are currently provided by large-scale, centralized, institutional technologies in most modern states.

Discussant's Remarks

David A. Goslin

In reflecting upon the perceptions and propositions advanced in the preceding chapters, five key issues or themes
come to my mind as being particularly worthy of discussion.
These issues merit special attention in this particular forum
because they represent prominent features of the context within which the family policy debate is taking place.

The first theme is one that runs through all of the preceding papers, and indeed reflects a great debate that is
going on throughout the United States at the present time.
This is the debate over freedom versus social control: free
market versus government regulation; private enterprise versus
big government; hands-off versus intervention; sink-or-swim
versus assistance/interference; provision of resources (e.g.,
money) versus provision of services (e.g., day care). At its
heart lies the question of the extent to which we should attempt to plan our future as opposed to letting it happen to
us.

In the context of this debate, which pervades almost
every aspect of public policy making in the United States,
there is enormous ambivalence about tampering with the family.
The family is a very private institution. We resist the idea
of interfering with it and with people's lives. This ambivalence is reflected in discussions, for instance, about day
care. Do we provide day care services for families or do we
give families money and let them purchase whatever services
they wish? I had the experience of helping a committee of the
National Academy of Sciences try to deal with this issue two
years ago and I assure you that it is not easily resolved.
Yet, at the same time that we consciously eschew actions that
are specifically designed to affect the family, we are increasingly forced to recognize that a great deal of government
policy affects families profoundly, as Professor Stack, I
think, amply demonstrates. Her conclusion, that the best way

to support families is to support individuals, seems to make a good deal of sense. It rests on an important basic assumption, however; namely, that individuals--at least individuals with resources--will, in fact, solve their own problems. This assumption--that the free market mechanism actually works--raises a number of subsidiary questions: How do we deal with substantial inequities in available resources? How do we ensure that consumers of goods and services have sufficient information to make wise choices? Under what circumstances are external controls necessary to protect individuals and families from potential dangers ranging from unsafe automobiles to mistreatment of children in day care centers? Attempts to answer each of these questions leads us back to government intervention and so the debate continues.

Professor Boulding also touched on the issue of freedom versus control when he observed that people like planning; but they do not like "being planned." He notes that with planning, far more people tend to "be planned" than do the planning. The free market of an unplanned, uncontrolled society, on the other hand, is not an unalloyed blessing. Among other things, for example, the free market gives people more choices, which leads me to my second theme, which is the problem of having too many choices.

Choices cause anxiety, at both the individual and the group level. Will we choose correctly for ourselves, for others? Will they choose correctly for themselves, for us? What if there is a conflict between us and them? We have more choices today than did previous generations, and this, it seems to me, is one of the sources of our anxiety and our problems in thinking about the family. Today, as individuals, we have choices about whether to get married, or not; whether to have children, or not; whether to remain married or not, whether to remarry, or not. Similarly, if we have children, we can now choose to have somebody else take care of them if we wish.

All of these choices give us problems. Professor Boulding notes that everything is fuzzy--dependent upon our perspectives. Professor Stack echoes with the statement, "don't try to define the family!" But where are we to find guidance in making our choices about how we shall live? An instruction that each person should "do his or her own thing" is not often very helpful, especially in the absence of information about the likely consequences of alternative behaviors or lifestyles for the individual or the family.

A couple of years ago, I, along with several others, including Bruno Bettelheim and Rosabeth Kantor, was participating

in a panel discussion on the future of the family at Tulane
University. There were several thousand students in the audi-
ence, and a great deal of the discussion centered around the
fact that we now have a lot of options; that we are pretty
much free to do, or to be, whatever we want in contemporary
American society. You can form a commune; you can have extended families; you do not have to get married, and so on.
During the discussion period, a young man--a student at Tulane
--stood up and said, plaintively, to this panel of distinguished experts, "Listen, I have a question. I just sort of
want to get married and have kids; is that all right?"

This anecdote leads me to my third basic theme or issue;
it stems from a word--a concept--that was not mentioned by any
of the preceding authors: <u>responsibility</u>. Who has it? Who
takes it? For what? How do we establish boundaries of individual responsibility? Who shall bear the responsibility
for the consequences of our choices, for their impacts on
others, on our children, our parents, other people in our
community? People, want, and (perhaps) need, to know how they
are supposed to behave, what they should be responsible for.

Professor Boulding pointed out that there seems to be a
natural desire to enlarge, to expand the family; that there is
always a drive for bigger families, moving from the nuclear
family, to the extended household, to the commune, to the
kibbutz, to society as a whole. Why, if this is true, is
there a desire to expand the family? Is it because we want to
diffuse responsibility? Are we seeking someone else to share
our responsibilities with us? Is that also the reason why we
tend to rely increasingly upon specialists to help us take
care of our children, to resolve our differences through coun-
seling or through the courts? Is this why we turn to social
workers or institutions when we cannot cope with our own kids?
Are we unwilling to accept responsibility? Have we created a
society where we are not prepared to take responsibility?

The issue of responsibility in contemporary society leads
directly to a fourth basic issue or theme within the context
of the family policy debate. This is the extraordinary increase in the role of law in our society during the past 10 or
15 years. It is not surprising to me in the context of the
points I have made already to note this continuing increase in
the influence of the legal system in our everyday life. If
we cannot define our responsibilities, or are unwilling to accept them, we have to turn to other institutions to do it for
us. Increasingly, we have been turning to the courts--and to
lawyers--to help us define our responsibilities.

For example, we see a great deal of attention now being given to the question of children's rights. Children's rights versus who else's rights? Adults' rights? Government responsibilities? We see a movement towards the development of marriage contracts before people get married, so that responsibilities are clearly stated, including what will happen if the marriage does not work out. But, again, there are a lot of unfortunate by-products from depending upon other institutions to solve our problems. Both the interjection of the courts, and the reliance upon the courts tend to make our decision-making processes adversarial, rather than cooperative and tend to define problems in "yes-no," "win-lose" terms, when, in reality, most questions have a broad range of possible solutions. Moreover, the well-publicized involvement of our legal system in our everyday lives tends to reinforce our propensities to use that system; to abdicate our own responsibilities: let the courts decide, let the social worker decide, let the psychiatrist decide, what is to be done.

Finally, my fifth theme concerns families as agents of socialization. Among other reasons, we are interested in families because we believe--correctly in my judgment--that they have a great deal of influence on the way the next generation is going to solve its problems. As Dr. Warnat has pointed out, we rely heavily on parents to instruct their children in how to solve problems; how to cope with choices. But if parents today cannot cope with the choices they themselves face, if they have too many options and do not know how to deal with them, then they may not be very good at teaching their kids how to cope with problems. My concern, therefore, about Professor Warnat's presentation is that I am not sure that many families can do all of the things that she is proposing for them to do. I think families have done them, in the past. I think that they ought to do them, but, as Urie Bronfenbrenner has pointed out, I am not sure that they can in the absence of an adequate system of social supports.

What may we conclude from the preceeding discussion? It seems unlikely to me that we will ever seriously attempt to reduce the number of options/choices available to individual members of society. Every current trend points in the opposite direction. Nor will we succeed in doing away with big government, Proposition 13 notwithstanding. Families increasingly will require assistance, of a variety of sorts, in carrying out their major functions. Most important, while we can expect continued diffusion of responsibility for the socialization of children, this must not be allowed to lead to abdication of responsibility, either on the part of the family or other social institutions, including both government and private industry. The family, whatever forms it may take,

remains the cornerstone of our society. As such, it is in all
our interests to take responsibility for ensuring its continued health and vitality.

Social Security in the Year 2000

8

How to Get There and Where Will We Be When We Do?

Joseph F. Coates

I recall when I was a small child that my then middle-aged working aunt had just become a participant in the social security system. She told me about the benefits she anticipated and how this was going to provide her with some kind of security in her old age. I also vividly recall acquiring my own magic number -- the equivalent of a secular rite of passage, the necessary step to making official my own first job as a teenager. The number marked an important transition in my life, or so it seemed.

The Social Security Administration has also brought me great news. That happened at a trade fair a year or so ago. At SSA's exhibit, a young lady was sitting at a computer console. If she was provided with your surname, she could tell you how many people with your name had been registered in the system since it started. I gave her my name. After several seconds she announced that some 25,000 people in the system are named Coates. Then I tried my wife's maiden name and found there were roughly a quarter of a million Taylors. Then I really tested it. I asked her how many Zilches there were, and the machine chomped away and came up with 619 Zilches. Then I put the console to the ultimate test. I gave another name; the console chomped away, and tick, tick, tick an answer came out. The young woman ripped it off and handed over what was the best news government has ever given to me. The message was that "There Is No Crud In The System."

Based upon a presentation to the Maryland Chapter of the American Society for Public Administration, which met at the Social Security Administration headquarters in Baltimore, Maryland on December 14, 1976.

These early and late good feelings toward the social
security system should not obscure the fact that the system
faces acute short-term problems and major long-term choices.

In discussing the long-term future of the social
security system and its administration, we skip over the
short-term problems -- such as financing, dwindling revenue
base, and increasing service demands -- in order not to have
our freedom of conjecture hampered by arguments and issues
which in the long-term context may turn out either to be
misperceived or relatively inconsequential. It is worth
notice, however, that such short-term problems have arisen,
since this very fact, about an enterprise almost uniquely
susceptible to usefully precise actuarial projection,
suggests the absence or at least the failure of long-range
planning. It also suggests, at a moment when we can see
relatively rapid change in demographic and other social
indicators, that a continued failure to address the future
is likely to lead to ever more defective decisions in efforts
to correct the clearly visible immediate problems.

Now, just how may we address the future of the social
security system in a meaningful way? Central to contemporary formal thought regarding the assessment of the future
for policy purposes is the concept of "alternative futures"
and I would propose here to examine several alternative
futures for the social security system. But before I do, I
believe it would be instructive to review the fundamental
rationale which underlies a futures analysis of this sort
since we are dealing here with a body of disciplines and
principles that is only recently coalescing into an orderly
field of study.

Alternative Futures

The first basic notion entertained by most serious
students of the future is that there are very real alternatives ahead of us. The future is not like a movie in which
the next frame is already in place and just waiting to be
revealed to us. Rather, an appropriate simile is one in
which the future is likened to the branching of a tree, in
which there are many branch points and many choices that can
be made. It is not like an oak tree or a walnut tree, but
it is more like a banyan tree. Some of the branches fall
back on each other, and you may even get a second pass if
you missed it the first time around. The concept of branching and critical branch points is central to thinking about
the future.

The <u>second</u> basic belief of most futurists is that we have the mechanisms and the means to see, to some useful extent, what those alternatives are. No one would make the claim that we can see precisely what the future is going to be in all of its detail. But futurists do make the well-substantiated claim that we can see the broad outlines of the alternatives ahead of us.

The <u>third</u> basic proposition is that we have the mechanisms and the means for steering and navigating civilization among and between those alternatives. While we cannot guarantee a good future, we believe that we have the means to assure that we are more likely to move away from the bad and toward the good.

And then <u>fourth</u>, is the proposition that almost all agree on, that we have a moral obligation to exercise our previously mentioned capabilities. By examining an institution's future in terms of those principles, we can achieve a structured, cogent anticipation of what may happen. As a minimum, that permits us to plan for and to accommodate to such steady changes and exigencies as the future may pose. But, accommodation is only one strategy. The much more interesting and exciting strategy is not just to prepare, but rather to begin to manipulate, to control, to influence, to mold the way that the future goes.

The principle strategy in beginning to probe the future is to look at long-range trends affecting the basic structural elements of the system with which we are concerned. By that I mean patterns of behavior -- patterns of institutional and individual behavior, patterns of social and economic behavior, and patterns of natural behavior -- which are relatively stable over a useful interval. Sometimes a useful interval is a couple of years; sometimes it is several decades. But the concept of long-range trends is central to looking at alternative futures, and when one looks at these long-range trends, one can identify them as boundary conditions -- constraints upon the future. One can also study long-range trends to advantage as forces through which existing constraints may break down or no longer hold; in other words, places where we may have a discontinuity in the future.

Discontinuity

Perhaps the most striking example of a sharp discontinuity in a trend in the past decade was the rapid change in the behavior of the OPEC countries over the price of oil. Clearly, that change surprised large segments of both the public

and private sectors. That is what I mean by discontinuity:
sudden, rapid change.

On the other hand, you can have other forms of change;
you can have a steady but clear movement in a new direction.
Perhaps an example of this would be the increasing entry of
women into the labor force or the growth of women's civil
rights activities. You may recall that there was a major
female civil rights movement around the time of World War I.
Trends can go up; they can go down; they can change. Understanding those steady, smooth changes and sharp discontinu-
ities is important in planning for the future.

Now, a key advantage one gets out of understanding these
trends is the identification of crucial points of intrusion
at which we can have an effect on how the future will unfold,
and at which we can act to use that trend to our advantage.
Let us turn now to some of these long-term trends and what
they imply for the future of the social security system.

Long-Term Trends

Clearly, a development of paramount relevance to the
social security system is the present long-term trend toward
an older population. I am sure that you are all aware of the
fact that we are experiencing an explosive growth of the
geriatric generation. That growth will continue. There are
forces in motion that may accelerate that trend. Major
research on aging gives us every reason to believe that life
can be extended. Voluntary changes in life style -- eating
habits, exercise, etc. -- already credited with a reduction
of some diseases, may also be expected to contribute to
longevity. The interesting question, of course, is:
"If life is extended by any significant number of years (let
us say 3, 5, or 7), where will that extension occur?" Will
the extension be more in old age or will the extension occur
in the middle years? Will you have a longer youth and middle
age, or will you have a longer period of decline and senility? Obviously these questions ought to be of major importance to the social security system. It is interesting to
me to note that the principal study of the implications of
life extension is not occurring in those agencies that are
promoting life extension through research. There is a lesson
there we ought to take to heart. Organizations often shut
their eyes and minds to both the potentially major effects of
their activities <u>and</u> the dominant factors influencing their
missions.

There is every reason to believe that drugs that prevent
senility in both the psychological and the physiological

sense are just around the corner. What are the implications
of that for the Social Security Administration?

Another long-term trend, as we move toward an aging
population, is a decline in the youthful population. And
what does that imply? The economic and labor burden of the
American society has largely been borne by men between ages
35 and 55. That is a fact, not a chauvinist statement.
Right now there are about 3.2 workers for every beneficiary.
Some extrapolations suggest that within the next 50 or 60
years we will have only two workers per beneficiary. What
does that mean? The least significant thing that it means
is that we will continue with business as usual. But more
likely, it implies major structural changes in order to
accommodate that basic new reality. I will suggest what
some of the changes may be.

The shift toward an older population implies a declining
work force. Assuming that we will continue to need goods and
services in order to sustain our economy, there are five
things we can do: (1) we can recruit new labor -- mostly
women, (2) we can start getting people in earlier and keep
them in the work force longer, (3) we can import new labor as
they are doing in Scandinavia and Germany, (4) we can increase
our dependence on foreign goods, or (5) we can increase
productivity. Each of these alternatives is, to some extent,
now being tried, and it is important to look at these options
because each has different implications for the Social
Security system.

Is the alternative to a declining work force increased
automation and capital intensivity, or does it mean drawing
more people into the labor market earlier and keeping them
longer? These questions need to be examined, not only in
the sense of organizational anticipation, but also in the
sense of defining reasonable public policy options. The
crucial question is whether it is in the public interest to
reverse, promote, or ignore the long-term trend toward
earlier retirement. Is it in the public interest to begin to
change the modal behavior of the aging worker? One cannot
answer that question without some analysis. Of course,
economic imperatives could amplify the demand for labor.
Capital intensivity, for example, may become less attractive
in the future for two reasons: first, competing global demands on capital and second, the high energy requirements of
capital intensive operations.

Thus, we might very well experience a natural reversal
of the previous long-term trend toward earlier retirement;
in contemplation of such an event, the key questions should

be: what are the policy levers, i.e., the government actions
or programs that might make delayed retirement socially useful
or socially significant? We are talking about trends that
are going to be continuous as well as trends that will
sneak up on us. If we do not think about the implications
of such trends, they will sneak up on us just as the recent
financial crisis did. Somebody has to begin to probe the
policy implications and the consequences of the kinds of
shifts in the structure of the work force that are implicit
in present trends.

Let me suggest that the salvation for the Social Security Administration (SSA) could possibly come from what
almost everyone else is seeing as the bête noire of the
economy, namely inflation. As the value of money declines,
the present and perhaps excessively large benefits the SSA
is delivering or promising to deliver will decline in relative importance. So one possible way out of SSA's future
dilemma would be stabilizing the benefit rates and letting
inflation chew away at the potential burden on the system.
I think one needs to look seriously at what the implications
of 20, 30, or 40 years of continuing inflation are. It would
be ironic, but the salvation of the Social Security Administration could arise from this widely deplored phenomena.

Change in the Aging

Most Americans now working will be candidates for the
benefits of social security by the turn of the century --
providing he or she is insured, of course. It would be
incorrect to presume that the aging and the aged in the year
2000 will be like the aging and the aged of today. A person
born in 1910 would be over 65 years old today. The chances
are that he is not even a high school graduate; that he has
gone through a major depression; that he has gone through one
major war in his adulthood and 2 or 3 substantial wars in
his lifetime. He has a mental set, view, or attitude toward
the world which in no way resembles values and beliefs of
today's young adults. On the other hand, the chances are
that, as today's early middle-aged cohort moves into retirement age at the turn of the century, it will at least have
completed high school, have a year or two of college, have
grown up in times of incredible prosperity, have assumed all
the middle class attitudes of high expectations, and most
significantly of all, will be accustomed to "jiggling" the
system. The passivity of those born in 1910 is literally
unknown to those born after 1935. Consider how many under
age 45 have participated in some kind of public protest or
public advocacy, marched, picketed, or paraded. The aged
of the turn of the next century are not going to be

content to supinely receive the benefits, abuse, ineptitude,
or fatuities of government. Rather, the system will be
mercilessly "hassled" by an educated, activist, participa-
tory geriatric generation.

SSA's Responsibility

Let me also suggest that, characteristic of the problems
of most public agencies, the elements of SSA's realm of
responsibility are largely and basically shaped by forces that
lie outside of its responsibility. To illustrate what I
mean, take the problem of disruption in the schools.
Clearly, the schools, school principals, and school systems
have virtually no control over housing policies, employment
policies, land use policies, or family income policies. Yet
the schools become the agencies most directly responsible
for coping with the resulting characteristics in the behavior
of children in the school system. Or, take the situation of
the police. It is well established that society gets very
little return by increasing the number of policemen or the
dollars per policeman who work on the street. Why? Because
crime is not squelched by the actions of the police, but is
undercut and prevented by the general temper and the general
conditions of society. So, in a similar way, the social
security system has responsibility for dealing with a sector-
ial problem in our society and in our economy over which it
exercises very little control.

One strategy for managing the future is to get a better
grasp of what the origins of your problems are and begin to
think of new and better ways for society to deal with them.
Now, what are the origins, the causes of, the major problems
confronting the social security system today? Well, of
course, there are demographic trends which we have already
discussed, which have contributed, and will continue to contribute, to the size of your constituency and the sheer
volume of their needs. But beyond this, what other factors
have made your mission more difficult than it was, say 30
years ago?

Certainly, it seems to me, altered family life-styles
have done much to increase the demands upon, and the expectations of the social security system. At the turn of the
century, people tended to have large households; not only
members of the immediate family, there were commonly lodgers,
boarders, immigrant relatives, and other adults in the household. That is pretty much passe now, for several reasons.
When people were living in rural areas, their homes were
often larger. When they moved to the city, where land costs
were high, houses tended to become smaller. The numbers of

children per household diminished too, as education levels
rose, as technology gave us better means of birth control,
as children ceased to be a form of old age insurance (in
part, due to social security), as educational aspirations
and costs rose, and as the requirements of suburban domestic
management made increasing demands on the time and energy of
the mother/housewife.

Not only have families and their dwellings become
smaller, but economic demands, and a freedom of individual
career aspirations, have resulted in increased family mobility,
so that today about 1 family in 5 moves each year. Extended
family networks, which once might have been scattered about
a single town, county, or even city, are now scattered
around the country, and beyond. Each new generation, if not
each new age cohort, pursues its own destinies, leaving
the parental generation behind. This appears to be particularly so today where the long-term decline in family size
is accelerated by the rise in divorce and single parent
households. And, with the almost explosive movement of women
into the labor force, the leverage of time economics upon the
commitments and availability of productive adult members of
our society grows greater each year.

In short, during the past 30 years, a combination of
trends has produced a predominance of small, largely ego-
centric, semi-nomadic household units in our society, with
neither physical, temporal, nor psychic space in their lives
for their parents or grandparents. And so, we have shifted
the burden of providing for the elderly to the public sector.
(It should not be overlooked, by the way, that the creation
of social security encouraged the evolution of the current
U.S. family life-style by implicitly promising that the aged
would be cared for and thus freeing the productive adults,
at least in part, of that concern.) Of course, other groups
in our society, whom the productive majority feel unable to
adequately support, are also consigned to public sector
responsibility; the retarded, the mentally ill, the handicapped are also commonly dealt with in this manner.

But, our concern here is for the aged, the constituency
of our social security system. And, if the demographic and
life-style trends I have been describing remain unaltered,
the social security system will almost certainly face a
continuing growth in public maintenance costs for the
elderly.

Now, an obvious alternative, an attractive one I
believe, would be to reintegrate the aging into family units.
In order to do this, we might "sweeten the kitty" for those

family units into which they would be integrated. How much
money would you want to take an aged grandmother, uncle,
aunt, or cousin back into the family? Would you do it for
$1,000 a year, $2,000 a year, $8,000 a year, $12,000 a year,
or $100,000 a year? What would be the individual and aggre-
gate cost in order to move people out of the nursing homes
and out of the individual hovels in which many of them are
living, and into comfortable accomodations with members of
their own family - children or grandchildren? How would the
costs compare with our current program costs, through Medicare, welfare, foodstamps, etc?

Until we make a serious effort to answer these kinds of
questions, we will not have begun to make a responsible
analysis of alternative policies for managing an aging population. But, while the assessment of so "radical" an alternative to current policy toward the elderly is outside the
scope of the Social Security Administration, it would seem
central to the agency's future. Somehow, we must begin to
look at this as a major alternative in dealing with problems
of the aged.

This is only one example, and obviously you can multiply
it in a number of different ways. One of the interesting
aspects for the future, of course, is to recognize that
government, in a short-term sense of largesse and political
benefit, has allowed the benefit and retirement programs to
get completely out of hand. Multiple programs, inchoate
programs, and clearly over-rewarding programs are now the
rule rather than the exception. For example, the military
officer is like the urban policeman. Both can retire at a
comfortable income at age 40 or 45. Well, at some point
along the way, when we had an army of 200,000 and we wanted
to keep those cadres functioning, it made sense. At some
time in the past, when the lives of urban policemen were perhaps shorter, or more threatened, it was important to have
young burly, physically vigorous people on the force. Gener-
ous retirements to promote turnover, perhaps made some sense.
But what happens is that these decisions of the past get
propagated into the present and into the future.

We must begin to address the question of restructuring
and reformulating the whole retirement system, not just a
piece of it. One can see that the expansion of pensions and
retirement systems in the federal and state governments and
in large areas of the private sector is in some social sense
getting out of hand. By that, I mean it is creating burdens
that are very probably unrealistic for the future. Now is
the time to begin to plan for dealing with them. If a solution is sought under crisis, it will probably only be a

larger and more expensive band-aid, such as the 1977 Social
Security Act.

Up to now, I have been discussing alternative futures
devolving from changing demographic patterns in our society.
The area of technology will also have interesting implications for the social security system. As I earlier suggested, the greater use of automation and reduced requirements
for physical strength and stamina in the workplace resulted
in the integration of women into jobs that were traditionally
only occupied by men: jobs in the machine shops, jobs on the
telephone lines, jobs in construction, and so forth and so
on, not to mention the movement into white-collar work.
Technology is making occupational egalitarianism a reality
in our society, and will obviously extend that egalitarianism
into making it possible and appropriate for the aging to work
longer at a greater diversity of jobs.

An Information Society

The significant long-term economic trend in our nation
today is our movement toward an information society. About
55% of the nation's work force is now in information in one
way or another -- generating it, packaging it, distributing
it, or handling it.

This movement toward an information society is accompanied by a continuing explosion in telecommunications
technology. That is going to have interesting implications
for the future. The first implication is that more people
will be moving into that sector. It will require, on the
average, a higher degree of education than most traditional
work did. This reinforces the point I made earlier about
increased participation and citizen intervention in the
system. As is well known, as education increases, voting
increases; as age increases, voting increases. So one can
see clear opportunities for more effective intrusion by
citizens into government affairs in general.

As we move into this information-oriented society,
however, other effects will occur. There will be much
more direct intervention because the technology will
permit more direct intervention into the actual day-to-day
working and operating of the system. The numerous cases
of alleged inequity that are laid before the social service
institutions by the people who have a gripe or grievance
about the system will undoubtedly undergo major changes in
the way they are received and how they are handled. Telecommunications will permit, and other forces will compel
the bureaucrats and civil servants to come into direct

contact with the people with whom they are dealing. The paper
shuffling will gradually end within the next 10 or 15 years.
That is going to have a powerful effect on the way bureaucracies operate.

One of the interesting side-effects of this, and I think
by and large a beneficial one, will be to wash away the gray-
ness of bureaucracy. The Social Security Administration is
one of the few major bureaucracies in government with a truly
uniform gray public image. When people begin to see individuals and interact with them, not only will there be that
initial turbulence of discovery but also there will be a
positive benefit of new rewards within the system. Joe Jones
and Jane Smith, who do their job well, will come to be recognized and appropriately rewarded. Charlie Brown, the
schlemiel of the system, will get extinguished, at least
occupationally. I think that public intervention in most
large institutions will obviously be disruptive in the short
run. However, not only is it inevitable, but also it will
benefit the social effectiveness of the system in the long
run. It will humanize the system and the work that goes on
in it.

The information society is premised on credit. A
society moving more and more into such things as electronic
funds transfer will put a higher premium on having people
readily identifiable through their whole lifetime. One of
the major candidate agencies for initiating that process is
the Social Security Administration. The implications of that
trend for the future, you may assume, is enormous and something that requires further examination. There are vast
benefits from a universal lifetime ID number and card. There
are also great risks. Let us think about them now, not then.

Possible New Clienteles

There are interesting opportunities in the future for
extending the social security system. One ought to begin
early to look at the system's possible new clienteles to see
what kinds of social functions could, should, might, or ought
to be performed, and what the policy levers are for that
performance. In a society in which divorce is rapidly becoming the mode rather than the exception, there are large numbers of adults making a transition in their lives. And there
are large numbers of children undergoing troublesome trans-
itions as well. With an interesting pattern of illegitimacy
already extant and apparently growing within our society,
with a decline in large families and with the desire for the
wherewithal to provide more resources per child, one wonders
whether children might not become a major new clientele; not

the child who is handicapped, not the child who is retarded,
but the child who is caught up in the turbulence of a no
family or a new family life-style. Does that present a new
market? Will the temporarily disabled be a new clientele?
There is more to being disabled than needing health insurance. Is that a market which is going to be met in the
future? Or might not the family, as a whole, become the
principal client of an expanded social security system,
administering an array of grants, payments or even loans, to
sustain various household members through unemployment,
through post-operative therapy, through career transition,
restorative sabbaticals, etc. These are questions that one
must begin to look at, to analyze, and assess via all the
well-developed but neglected levels of analysis, information,
public participation and experimentation.

Some Other Developments

Before closing, it may be useful to suggest some other
long-term trends and possible developments which should concern the long-range planning of the Social Security Administration.

Work and Leisure

George Bernard Shaw was right on the mark when he
suggested that it's a pity youth is wasted on the young. As
the population becomes more educated and acquires more general middle class values of self-fulfillment, people will
demand changes to meet their humane rather than their simple
economic requirements. One of those may be for more work,
for better work, for more autonomous work, for more intri-
cately scheduled work and leisure over a whole working life.
That will be a very real factor in the future.

There is no meaningful answer to the question of what
will be the required work force in the years 1990 to 2000.
The question rather should be what are the alternatives? One
then begins to see which way we can steer; we can then see
which way we want to steer. In the future, rather than having a single extrapolation of work, we should have a branched
extrapolation. We should decide which branches we like, and
then what has to be done to get us there.

Crime and Information

One of the "neat" crimes for the future will be to
receive multiple benefits. Why not retire four times? I
presume it would be a fairly straightforward thing to retire
four times under the name of John Smith, Charles Jones, and

so forth. Right now we see, as we move toward an automated
society, that a clever and bright person could begin at age
50 or 40 or 30 to lay his future requirements for multiple
retirements into the computer system. There is a fasci-
nating court case involving relatively low level workers in
a large private commercial data bank. As I understand it
from the press, they were adjusting credit ratings for a fee
of, as I recall, anywhere from $150 to $1,500. Their organization carried information on millions of people, and gave
out information annually on 10 million. If I recall the
number correctly, they had "jiggered" some 5,000 credit
ratings. If you put those numbers together -- some 5,000
times a thousand dollars -- there is a tremendous "take" for
the one who can manipulate the system. As we move into an
information society, not only the attractiveness but also
the feasibility of manipulating the system in criminal or
semi-criminal ways will increase. We are not going to get
away from the abuse-of-information problem by saying, "It's
someone else's problem." The Social Security system, like
every other system of benefits, will be exposed to it. Is
there a counter-intelligence division looking at the un-
folding criminogenic aspects of the social security system?

It is highly likely that we will have an identification
card and number in the not too distant future. It seems to
me that the question for the Social Security Administration
is what should its proper relationship be to the card. We
should not let it spring up casually and be wished upon us.
The whole question of privacy and crime ought to be examined
carefully now in future terms.

Experimentation

Most of the major alternative institutional choices
facing us cannot adequately be probed by conjecture alone.
They cannot adequately be probed by assembling information.
They cannot adequately be probed even by analysis or
modeling. Many of the most interesting options and alternatives ahead of us can be effectively examined only by
trying them out. A major institutional innovation in the
public interest would be to define and set up a series of
what I call "intervention experiments." Go out there to
the people and run real experiments, with real people on
a large enough scale for a long enough time so that you
really learn what options work and what options do not.
Until one moves to that kind of experimental approach
toward public policy formulation, we are going to continue
to flounder.

This idea is not without precedent. We now have

major experiments in income maintenance. They are revealing
beautiful things. The poor are not depraved. When you give
them resources, they use them wisely. "Performance contract-
ing" and voucher experiments in education are beginning to
reveal fundamental new information about those public policy
areas. One could usefully define a half dozen major experiments of this intervention nature that the Social Security
Administration should be sponsoring and conducting. These
experiments are not going to be possible within the present
framework of activities. In some cases, it will be necessary
to ask for major exceptions from regulations or from institutional constraints -- regulatory "holidays" to encourage
social enterprise, similar to the tax "holidays" granted by
many political jurisdictions to encourage commercial enterprise. All kinds of special things will have to be re-
quested, but when one examines the alternatives ahead of
us it should be clear that experiments have the potential
of being major tools in forming critically needed new public
policy.